To Frank & Jane
with best regards

Jay Fast

California Orange Box Labels

AN ILLUSTRATED HISTORY

By Gordon T. McClelland and Jay T. Last

Hillcrest Press, Inc. P.O. Box 10636, Beverly Hills, California 90210 U.S.A.

© Hillcrest Press, Inc., 1985
ISBN   0-914589-01-6
Library of Congress Catalog Card Number
84-082283

Hillcrest Press, Inc.
P.O. Box 10636
Beverly Hills, California 90210

Design by Hyatt Moore
Art Production by Meredith Bradbury
Label photographs by Mike Rupp

Printed and Bound in Japan by Dai Nippon
Typography by Thompson Type, San Diego

TABLE OF CONTENTS

INTRODUCTION

In the seventy year period from the 1880's to the mid 1950's millions of colorful paper labels were used by California citrus growers to identify and advertise the wooden boxes of oranges they shipped throughout the United States. These labels provide a social history, a history of commercial art, and a history of California business. They are of increasing interest to collectors today because of their attractive designs and interesting subject matter.

Oranges were first grown in California in the late 1700's, brought from Mexico by the Spanish colonists. The cultivation of oranges gradually increased as the population grew and as new areas were found which had satisfactory soil and climate. For the first eighty years of orange cultivation, Southern California had no easy way to communicate with the rest of the country; oranges were grown mainly for local consumption.

The construction of the Southern Pacific and Santa Fe railroads in the late 1870's and early 1880's linked Southern California to the rest of the continent. This provided an eastern market for the fruit, and led to a rapid influx of new settlers who recognized the agricultural promise of the state. Many settled in rural areas and planted orange groves.

These early growers were presented with a class of problems that had never been faced on this scale before—how to pack, ship, identify and advertise a perishable product for customers who lived thousands of miles away. The brightly colored, attractively designed paper label proved to be a key ingredient in the solution of this problem.

A great deal of experimentation took place in the early years to develop and label a satisfactory shipping container. The basket and barrel used for eastern agricultural produce, such as apples, was not satisfactory for railroad shipment. A rectangular box that could be easily handled and efficiently packed in railroad cars was developed, as shown on the *Riverside* label.

The first boxes were labeled by branded trademarks or stencilled images. The earliest surviving labels are small circular paper images about 6" in diameter, which were pasted in the center of a rectangular stencilled pattern. They were quickly superseded by large paper labels, about 11" x 10", pasted on the ends of rectangular boxes. The dimensions of these orange box labels did not change for the next 70 years.

Their purpose—to rapidly catch the attention and interest of prospective purchasers—was the same as for advertising posters developed in the 1880's and 1890's. In the hands of a good artist and graphic designer, the orange box label became an

elegant small poster, containing an easily understood and remembered message.

The effect of this graphic image was strengthened when the labels were seen on stacked arrays of boxes in the eastern wholesale houses. In contrast to most product advertising, the labels were not directed toward the ultimate consumer, but were intended for the wholesale buyer who quickly made decisions among a variety of competing brands. The serial image effect was an effective sales tool.

The first labels were produced by stone lithography, by sequentially printing up to six colors to form the final image. Color lithographic techniques needed for the production of these graphic images were well developed by this time, having first been used in the 1860's in the eastern United States for posters and large tobacco box labels. The California printing industry, which produced nearly all the orange box labels, was located in San Francisco and Los Angeles. In the twentieth century, stone lithographic techniques were gradually replaced by photocomposition processes and offset printing.

While the external dimensions and product identification requirements for labels remained unchanged for the seven decades of label use, the specific art treatment used gradually evolved, reflecting new advertising concepts, design themes, and production techniques. A chronological survey of orange box labels provides an encapsulated history of American commercial art during this period.

A label often was used for decades if it proved to have an easily remembered title and successful graphic image. While the introduction of new labels was usually slow and evolutionary, the use of new label themes and design concepts can be divided into three distinct periods.

The first period—thirty-five years from the mid-1880's until the end of World War I—was one in which the treatment of label themes and designs from a naturalistic point of view predominated, in line with American popular art of the period. Flowers, birds, animals, historical themes and scenic views were treated in profusion.

A change took place about 1920, along with the transition in America from a predominantly rural to an urban society and an increased emphasis on product advertising. The orange box labels began to stress the benefits to health and well-being from eating oranges and drinking orange juice. New eye-catching designs, new label themes, and innovative use of color were employed.

The final period, from the mid 1930's until the mid 1950's, featured designs based on commercial art school concepts, using graphic product identification techniques, such as dramatic sloping block lettering.

The use of paper labels ended abruptly in the mid 1950's, when cardboard cartons replaced the wood boxes. Wood had become more expensive, the cost of labor for assembling boxes rose, and cardboard containers were developed which were strong enough to survive severe shipping conditions. The new cardboard boxes contained simple product identification designs preprinted on the box ends. In 70 years, the labeling of orange boxes had come full circle, from the simple brand identification on boxes in the 1880's to the simple printed labels on cardboard boxes today.

During the period of label use, over 8000 distinct designs were developed, and used on over two billion boxes of oranges. There were many minor variations on these basic images due to different label printers, change of ownership of the brand name, and the incorporation of special product and trademark information. The inclusion of these variations increases the number of label designs to at least 15,000.

Label artists often considered their work to be a less prestigious aspect of commercial art than the design of magazine covers or national product advertisements. Since label design was often a joint project, and since many lithographic companies had restrictions against signed work, practically no label designs bear the artist's signature. In spite of this anonymity over 50 label artists have been identified, and their work discussed here. Considered at the time it was created as just one of many commercial design tasks, label art has steadily increased in interest, until today it is one of the most appreciated aspects of early commercial art.

Considering that orange box labels were discarded after use, it is remarkable that so many survive. Most early labels still in existence are ones that were kept in government and industry trademark and patent files, in salesmen's sample books, and in printing house archives. Also, because they were so colorful and attractive in an era when printed material was not nearly as common as today, a number of private label collections were assembled in California, beginning about 1900. Few labels soaked off the boxes have survived.

Most early labels are rare—several of those illustrated here are the only existing examples. Few early labels exist in quantities of more than 25.

Later labels exist in larger quantities, however. With the rapid replacement of wooden boxes and paper labels by cardboard boxes in the 1950's, large numbers of unused labels remained in packing houses. Many were gathered up and saved. They form a large body of material available to persons interested in collecting and studying this graphic form of American commercial art—the elegant small poster.

Naturalism (1885-1920)

Advertising (1920-1935)

Commercial Art (1935-1955)

HOME BRAND

GROWN AND PACKED BY
R.A.EDDY,

HIGH GROVE,
CALIFORNIA.

CHAPTER I
NATURALISM (1885-1920)

Most of the early California citrus growers were newcomers to the state, having arrived from the eastern United States or from Europe as young adults, or as older businessmen who were intrigued with the idea of living their retirement years in a California orange grove.

They had many initial problems to surmount—first, the purchase of satisfactory orchard land, often dealing with unscrupulous land salesmen known locally as "escrow Indians," who were not above tying oranges on Joshua trees and trying to sell desert lands as orange groves. The growers had to determine which varieties of oranges would grow well in their area, and had to solve the problems of adequate water supplies, the all-too-common winter frosts, troublesome plant diseases and insects.

After successfully solving or circumventing these problems and producing a crop, the citrus grower realized his task had just begun. He had to sell the oranges. This involved complex interactions among growers, packers, shippers, railroad agents, eastern wholesale jobbers, retail fruit stores and, finally, consumers. The orange box label played a key role in this communication process.

After experimenting with a variety of containers and branding and stencilling techniques, the rectangular wooden shipping box was developed about 1885, with a paper label about 11″ x 10″ attached to one end. This identifying label gave the brand name, the shipper's or packer's name and address, and an attractive image in the form of a small poster.

Little attempt was made to advertise the quality of the fruit or to promote the use of oranges. The purpose of the label was to provide an eye-catching way to identify the fruit for eastern produce dealers, who would, hopefully, remember the brand name and image and reorder.

The subject matter of early labels reflected the popular art of the period—naturalistic treatment of everyday subjects. At this time, chromolithographs produced in large quantities by Currier and Ives and by Louis Prang were widely sold. Early label subjects—California scenery, pioneer heroes, Indians, flowers, birds and animals—fit into this model.

Early growers took a strong interest and pride in their new Southern California home and in their newly planted orange groves. Their labels often featured personal themes like their homes and families, as well as scenes of orange growing and harvesting.

MAGIC ISLE BRAND

PACKED BY
G.R. HAND & COMPANY,
CALIFORNIA

PARENT TREE BRAND

PACKED BY STRACHAN FRUIT CO., SUCCESSORS
G.R. HAND & COMPANY, CALIFORNIA.

ECHO BRAND

GROWN and PACKED BY
PASADENA
ORANGE GROWERS' ASSOCIATION
PASADENA, CALIFORNIA.

LOS ANGELES COUNTY.

ARROYO BRAND

GROWN and PACKED BY
PASADENA ORANGE GROWERS' ASSOCIATION
PASADENA, LOS ANGELES CO., CALIFORNIA.

Tournament BRAND.

NEW-YEAR'S-DAY'S
ANNUAL TOURNAMENT OF ROSES
PASADENA, CAL.

GROWN AND PACKED BY
PASADENA ORANGE GROWERS' ASSOCIATION,
PASADENA, CALIFORNIA.

OLD BALDY BRAND

CALIFORNIA
CITRUS
UNION.

CALIFORNIA

10

Southern California Scenes

Many early labels showed California scenery, featuring orange groves with snow capped peaks in the background. Palm trees, a novelty to many of the early growers, often appeared. Although these scenes were portrayed in attractive and colorful ways in early labels, the orchard and mountain theme soon became overused and stereotyped.

Specific turn-of-the-century scenes and events were illustrated on many labels. *Magic Isle* shows Avalon Harbor on Catalina Island, a resort off the California coast. *Parent Tree* is the first navel tree planted in Riverside in 1874, depicted after it was replanted with the help of President Theodore Roosevelt in 1903. The new bridge connecting two residential areas of Pasadena is shown in *Arroyo*. *Old Baldy* shows Upland's Euclid Avenue, a wide street leading to 11,000' snow capped Mt. Baldy in the background.

Echo shows the Mount Lowe inclined railroad, a popular excursion spot in the hills above Pasadena. This could be reached from many points in Southern California by the recently constructed interurban street car line, also shown. A flower bedecked carriage from Pasadena's first Rose Parade in 1889 is featured on *Tournament*.

As the orange industry became larger and geographically widespread, label themes became less specific. Depictions of local scenes and events became less common.

The Mexican Heritage

Southern California was first settled by Spanish colonists from Mexico in 1781, who established pueblos at San Gabriel and Los Angeles. A key element in the expansion of these settlements was the construction of a series of missions, roughly a day's journey apart, which stretched from San Diego to San Francisco. After Mexico gained its independence from Spain in 1822, the California mission system was abandoned and its buildings fell into ruin.

The early citrus growers were interested in this Spanish-Mexican culture in which they found themselves—and which they were busy changing. As interest in the role of the early missions developed in the later part of the 1880's, many were restored. Mission buildings and scenes of mission life were the subject of many early labels.

Other aspects of Mexican culture also appeared on labels. Vaqueros, the Mexican cowboys, were shown on many attractive labels, as were the dancing and pageantry associated with Mexican festivals, such as the Cinco de Mayo celebrations. Mexican themes remained favorite subjects throughout the years.

Names given to geographical features by the early Spanish explorers, and names from Mexican land grants and settlements still are prominent in Southern California. They have steadily appeared as label themes and titles, along with other Spanish words and phrases.

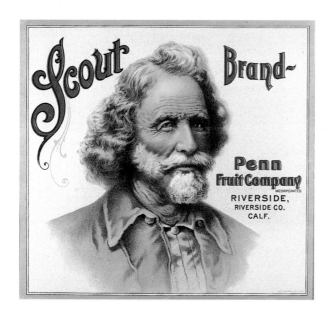

The Old West

The American frontier had disappeared for all practical purposes by the turn of the century, but popular heroes of the time were still the pioneers, the cowboys, the miners, and the cavalrymen who had tamed and developed the West. Labels showed them in active naturalistic situations.

Bronco and *Advance* are dramatic scenes from paintings by H.W. Hansen, a prominent Western artist employed in the 1890's by Crocker Lithograph in San Francisco.

Scout is a portrait of Buffalo Bill Cody, an early buffalo hunter famous in this period for his traveling Wild West shows. *Buffalo Bill*, a rare example of a label with an ornate border treatment, is reminiscent of the valentines of the time. It was printed in New York by McLaughlin Brothers, well known for their children's books and elaborate game boards.

Crack Shot is a powerful visual image. A stack of boxes adorned with this label would certainly have called attention to the brand.

While mining was quickly supplanted by agriculture as the main California commercial pursuit, the presumably glamorous lives of gold miners and prospectors remained a favorite label subject for years.

The Spanish-American War of 1898, with the well publicized exploits of Teddy Roosevelt's Rough Riders, furnished the subjects for a number of labels.

15

Indians

Indians and scenes of Indian life were often portrayed in American art during the 1800's. Charles Bird King, George Catlin, and Karl Bodmer painted numerous realistic portraits of Indians in the first half of the century, which were exhibited and published in book form.

Later in the century, a more stereotyped image developed, made famous by the popularity of dime novels with garish cover illustrations, and by the traveling Wild West shows of Buffalo Bill Cody. Publicity accompanying these shows usually depicted Plains Indians, often on horseback, wearing feathered war bonnets, beads, and colorful blankets.

These stylized representations, on millions of posters and advertisements promoting the Buffalo Bill shows, served as the model for most Indians depicted on orange box labels. While the scenes and costumes were not especially true to life, the treatment was usually dignified, showing Indians in scenes ranging from mountain lakes to inhospitable deserts.

The Pomona-Riverside area, location of many of the early groves, had been the site of numerous Indian settlements. The Indian Hill Citrus Association, founded in Pomona in the late 1880's, steadily used Indian themes, often in an orchard context.

Indians remained a much used label subject throughout the years. *First American* (page 69) was used as a title for over 50 years, as was the *Indian Hill* trademark shown here.

17

Patriotic Themes

Themes from colonial history were popular in American art before World War I. America, little more than a century old as a nation, was still close to its colonial and revolutionary heritage. There were more outward signs of patriotism than there are today, with Fourth of July parades, political slogans and banners, and patriotic advertisements and displays of all sorts.

America was finding its place in the world as an international power, with strong feelings of national pride and identity. The country was populated with large numbers of immigrants and new citizens, who had chosen America for its economic opportunities and political freedom.

Among the labels illustrating events from American history were the M.E. Ginn series of *Pilgrim, Tea Party,* and *Paul Revere.* These labels were printed by the Boston Banknote Company, one of the few label sets produced by a New England concern. *Yankee Doodle,* "The Spirit of 1776," is taken from a famous painting by Archibald M. Willard.

The American flag, the eagle, and girls draped in patriotic colors often were depicted on early labels. The *Salisbury Fruit Co.* label went the limit: it included a spray of orange blossoms with the flag, and an eagle sitting on a large orange.

Women

Without doubt, images of attractive women have been the most popular theme in advertising art throughout the years. Orange box labels were no exception. Women were on the earliest labels and continued to appear on them until the last labels used in the 1950's. Most of the early subjects were naturalistic portraits of actual people. Many showed women in conjunction with flowers or, as in *Our Popular*, part of a flower design.

While some labels depicted women as mythological goddesses dressed in flowing robes, or as patriotic figures draped in flags and bunting, most showed women tastefully dressed in contemporary clothing. They were often holding baskets or trays of oranges, or were in orchard scenes. In a number of well designed labels, as in *Sunshine*, women appeared in formal poses in front of landscapes.

A few labels showed women in exotic dress. *Gypsy Queen* is a striking portrait, done in 1891. The subject matter of *Maori Maids Greeting* is unique. The impetus for the label may have come from one of the international exhibitions held in America during this time. With the opening of Japan to Western trade in the 1850's, interest in Japanese themes developed, as in *Geisha*.

Birds and Animals

Hundreds of labels during this time featured birds and animals. Birds lent themselves naturally to label design, with their strong colors and easily identified images. Soaring birds, in particular, increased the dynamic feeling of the designs. While nearly all labels depicted birds in a naturalistic way, three outstanding exceptions exist. *Red Raven*, *Red Owl* and *Stork* are powerful labels, with flat images and bright colors.

Labels depicting animals ranged from docile household pets to exotic African beasts. Dogs appeared on many labels, in a variety of contexts. Domesticated cats were seldom shown; *Angora* is a rare exception. Wild animals usually were shown in placid, non-threatening poses. *Wolf* is an obvious exception; the designer seems to have lost sight of the fact that the purpose of the label was to sell oranges, accomplished by presenting an attractive sympathetic image.

In addition to the lion and tiger shown here, zebras, camels, and elephants were illustrated. See *Elephant* (page 78) pushing a giant orange.

As can be seen from these examples, most label titles in this naturalistic period were simple, direct descriptions of the subject. This reinforced the main purpose of the label—to identify the brand in a graphic, easily remembered manner.

Eagle Brand

ONTARIO CUCAMONGA FRUIT EXCHANGE — California

TRADE FAY MARK

SKY-HIGH BRAND

FAY FRUIT CO.

CALIFORNIA.

Swan Brand

REDLANDS FRUIT ASS'N.

GROWN and PACKED AT REDLANDS.

SAN BERNARDINO CO., CALIFORNIA.

WASHINGTON NAVELS

PARROT BRAND

SAN ANTONIO FRUIT EXCHANGE POMONA, CAL.

GROWN and PACKED BY POMONA FRUIT GROWERS EXCHANGE POMONA, Los Angeles County, Cal.

Robin Brand

FRUIT SHIPPERS SPENCE FRUIT CO. CALIFORNIA

OATMAN'S BLACK BIRD BRAND

E.J. OATMAN RIVERSIDE.

GROWN AT HIGHGROVE, CALIFORNIA.

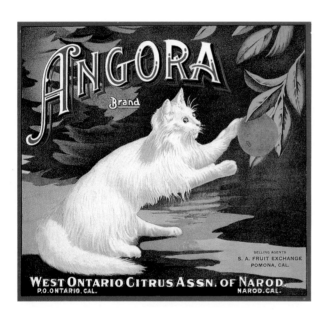

FAMILY BRAND

GROWN AND PACKED BY
ORANGE HEIGHTS FRUIT ASSOCIATION
CORONA,
RIVERSIDE CO., CALIFORNIA.

DOG BRAND

Redlands Oranges

GROWN AND PACKED BY
DREW FRUIT ASS'N.
REDLANDS, SAN BERNARDINO CO. CAL.

BLACK BEAUTY BRAND
EXTRA
FANCY ORANGES

WILLIAM HILLS
CALIFORNIA

STAG BRAND

Glendora   Oranges

Grown and Packed at
GLENDORA
LOS ANGELES COUNTY
CALIFORNIA

SHIPPED BY
AZUSA-COVINA-GLENDORA
FRUIT EXCHANGE
Azusa, California.

TIGER HEAD BRAND.

REDLANDS,
SAN BERNARDINO COUNTY,   CALIFORNIA.

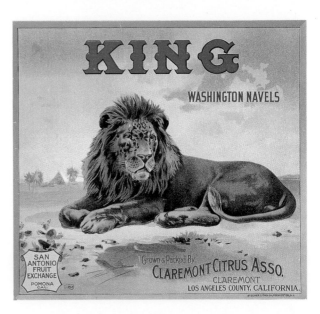

KING

WASHINGTON NAVELS

SAN ANTONIO FRUIT EXCHANGE
POMONA CAL.

Grown & Packed By
CLAREMONT CITRUS ASSO.
CLAREMONT
LOS ANGELES COUNTY, CALIFORNIA.

Flowers

Chromolithographic reproductions of flowers were very popular in turn-of-the-century America. Magazines often featured them as centerfolds, to be removed and framed. Currier and Ives produced a number of colorful fruit and flower designs, along with their naturalistic scenes of 19th century American life.

Flowers were an ideal subject for orange box labels. The pleasant colorful images conveyed an impression of wholesomeness and freshness that orange shippers wanted for their products. Since many oranges were sold during the winter, colorful designs were certainly a welcome sight in the eastern United States.

Flowers were grown in California year-round. Many of the roads winding through the orange groves were lined with flowers. In 1889, the city of Pasadena began to sponsor the Rose Parade, which gave flower growers from surrounding areas the opportunity to display their prize roses and other flowers. This emphasis on flowers in California life made it a popular choice for an orange grower selecting his label design.

Paul deLongpre, a California artist, became famous at this time for his paintings of floral arrangements. Many of his paintings were published by Louis Prang, the well known Boston chromolithographer. While there is no evidence that deLongpre was directly associated with the design of orange box labels, his flower images certainly influenced label designers.

Poster Influences

A few outstanding labels departed markedly from the common naturalistic designs discussed up to this point. They were inspired by the upsurge of interest in posters and poster collecting in the 1890's, in Europe and America. The realization that the poster was a new means of communication where the message had to be grasped quickly led many artists to experiment with new simplified design concepts.

Emerald and *Topaz* were inspired by the Art Nouveau designs of Alphonse Moucha. Characterized by hard edge designs, ornate curved lines, and flat, bold color, Art Nouveau had a marked effect on advertising art and early twentieth century design.

Gaiety and *La Belle* reflect the lighter design treatment of Jules Cheret and Henri de Toulouse-Lautrec, who produced posters for Parisian music halls such as the Moulin Rouge. They played key roles in the development of the posters as a fine art form.

La Fiesta was taken from a poster designed by Los Angeles artist M.E. Curran for the Los Angeles Fiesta celebration in 1897. The poster was used in railroad advertising, to encourage tourists to visit California.

Buscada was a most unusual label for the naturalistic period. It must have made a marked impression when it arrived in the eastern produce houses, seen in conjunction with standard orchard and mountain scenes.

LA-LOMA QUEEN

HIGHGROVE, CAL.
Riverside County

Spruance
Fruit Comp'y
California

PACKED BY

Hasson Bros. Co
CALIFORNIA.

CALIFORNIA CITRUS UNION

CALIFORNIA

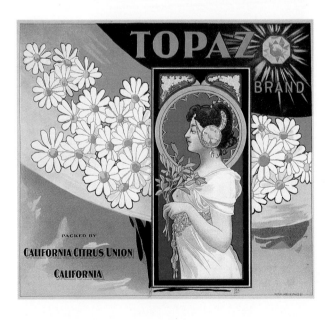

PACKED BY

CALIFORNIA CITRUS UNION

CALIFORNIA

SPRUANCE
FRUIT COMPANY
California

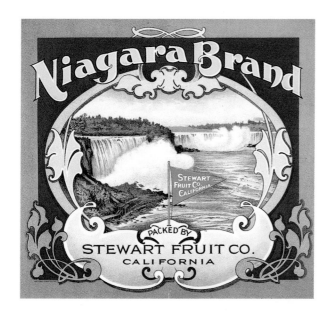

Commercial Shippers

Before the organization of successful growers' cooperatives in the early 1900's, such as the California Fruit Growers Exchange, many oranges were sold by commercial shippers in the Riverside and Los Angeles areas. These independent dealers recognized the importance of firm name and brand name recognition. They commissioned some of the best labels ever produced, often incorporating unifying themes in their designs.

An excellent series of labels with a unifying theme are the G.R. Hand labels, featuring a red triangle trademark. *Pyramid* with the pyramid and red trademark complementing each other, is especially well composed. *Magic Isle* and *Parent Tree* (page 10) also are Hand labels.

The Fay Fruit Company used a Maltese Cross trademark, emphasizing the theme of being a winner. The Steward Fruit Company showed water in violent motion, as in *Niagara* and *Rescue*, undoubtedly designed by the same artist.

The Porter Brothers commissioned some outstanding labels with dramatic images rather than prominent trademarks, as shown by *Klondike* and *Porter Brothers*.

Other commercial shipper trademarks were the Earl Fruit Company banner, shown on *Sunflower* (page 26) and *Yosemite* (page 88), and the Spruance diamond, shown on *Emerald* and *Amethyst* (page 29).

32

Stock Labels

In addition to designing and printing labels for specific customers, most early lithographers produced general purpose stock labels, with an area left blank for inserting the brand name and grower's address. A grower could purchase a stock label, and then have his brand information quickly incorporated on the label by local letterpress printers.

These labels filled a number of needs. A small grower could have a label of reasonably good quality at a low price. A grower, whose fruit at times was of inferior quality, could switch to a different brand name and dispose of the fruit without harming his regular brand name reputation. Growers who, for one reason or another, ran out of their supply of regular labels when they had fruit ready to ship, could put their brand name on a stock label, and maintain their product identification.

The hundreds of stock label designs produced prior to 1920 were used by many different growers and imprinted with a variety of label titles. This combination of different brand names and stock label designs adds greatly to the number of distinct labels that were created. Undoubtedly, a large number of these overprinted stock labels were used for a single shipment, and examples of the specific combination of label subject and brand title no longer exist.

"STRICTLY FANCY"

PACKED BY
WORTHLEY & STRONG
Riverside, Cal.

FREEDOM BRAND

"Arbutus"

FAY FRUIT CO.
CALIFORNIA.

CHAPTER II
ADVERTISING (1920-1935)

America underwent abrupt social changes in the years following World War I, from the ideas and conventions of a predominantly rural society to the faster paced, more sophisticated life of the city.

Exciting new modes of communication and transportation rapidly developed during the 1920's. Commercial radio broadcasting began near the start of the decade, bringing presidential election results and championship prize fights directly into the American home. Lindberg made his solo flight across the Atlantic in 1927, the most exciting event of the decade. The number of automobiles in the United States increased fourfold in the 1920's; by 1930 one in five Americans owned a car, and could use it on the rapidly expanding highway system.

This increased mobility and broader viewpoint led Americans to reassess their role in this exciting new world. There was a new emphasis on the good life, on youth, energy, health, and moral freedom.

More and more products were advertised and distributed nationally, increasing the number of potential customers, but also increasing the number of business competitors and rivals. Effective product identification and advertising became more important than ever for business success.

California citrus shippers, faced with problems of national distribution since the beginnings of the industry, had long realized the importance of product identification and advertising. The California Fruit Growers Exchange, the key growers cooperative, ran its first national advertisement in 1914, in the Saturday Evening Post. In the next two years, advertisements were placed in over 500 daily newspapers and more than a dozen national magazines.

The key person associated with this increased emphasis on advertising was Don Francisco, who was 24 when he became advertising manager of the California Fruit Growers Association in 1916. He brought a fresh and innovative approach to the promotion of California citrus fruit.

In addition to newspaper and periodical advertisements, recipe books, and posters on billboards and in streetcars, Francisco took a strong interest in the quality of the box labels, from the standpoint of their sales and advertising potential. Realizing that naturalistic label designs in use at the time had serious shortcomings, he wrote a booklet in 1918 entitled Labels—Suggestions for the shipper who is seeking to give his pack a worthy and effective mark of identification.

He pointed out that the label and label trademark had a tangible value, just as the orchard and packing house had value. He

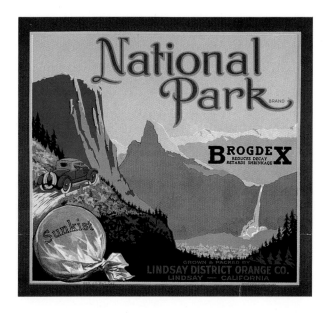

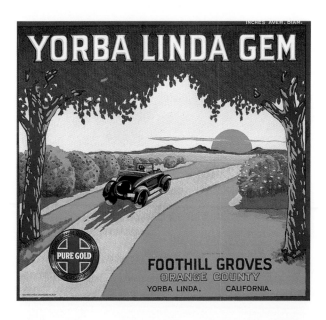

37

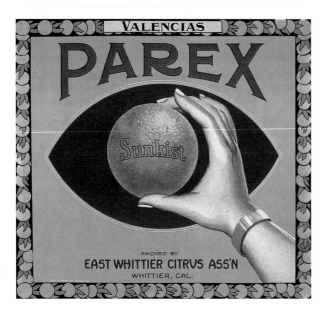

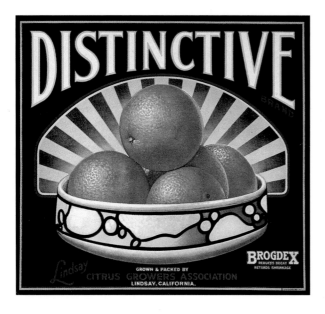

criticized labels in use at the time, and made many suggestions that influenced their design in the early 1920's. His suggestions are well understood today, but at that time they were new and innovative. He discussed the following points.

The label should be designed and the brand name selected with the buyer in mind. An effective label should be designed with the eastern wholesale jobber in mind. The jobber, rather than the retailer or the ultimate consumer, is the one who selects the fruit for distribution. A label which depends on some clever name or local fact known only in the California shippers community is not effective for the jobber who leads a different life in different surroundings. Even though most shippers have a secret desire to have pictures of their orange groves, their homes, or their families on their label, they should realize that if they cater to anyone's pride and vanity, it should be that of the buyer.

The brand name should be short, and both the brand name and the label should be simple. In the eastern produce markets and auction display rooms, the label must tell its story quickly. The general effect is more important than fine details. The color scheme and lettering should be simple, clear, and easily recognizable at a distance. The best way to judge a label is to stand it up and look at it from a distance of about 10 feet, since this most closely approximates the distance from which the jobber chooses his purchases.

The label and brand name should be distinctive. The fundamental object of the trade name and label is to distinguish it from similar, competing packages of fruit. Commonplace subjects such as orange groves and sprays of fruit should be avoided. Also the brand name should not include common over-worked words such as *Sunny Heights*. The image should illustrate the same idea that is expressed in the brand name.

The label should suggest the contents of the package. Comparatively few orange labels suggest the kind of merchandise in the box. The label will have added value if, by word or illustration, or both, it shows unmistakably what is inside.

The label should be pleasing and artistic. The public has become accustomed to high-class illustrative art, and clumsily handled designs make a bad impression. An inartistic design is jarring. The name should suggest value and worth, to add to the product's desirability. Labels should be serious, not absurd or degrading, unless a joke can drive home a pertinent selling point.

The label or brand name should suggest the source of the fruit. With heavy Sunkist advertising, the fact that the fruit comes from California should be featured. This will aid in the competition with fruit from Florida and Puerto Rico.

While older labels often were used for years or decades, new label designs, suggested by Don Francisco's marketing ideas and by changing American tastes, were introduced in the early 1920's. They focused on direct advertising and clear sales themes, and formed an innovative body of new subjects and designs.

These new labels emphasized the essentials of successful posters—clear simple images, forceful titles, and direct messages. It was accepted that a label was not a piece of art to be exhibited and admired for years, but rather an advertising message that had to sell its product in a few seconds in a competitive marketplace, while eliciting friendly and sympathetic customer reactions.

Oranges for Health

Orange producers realized the most effective way to increase the number of oranges sold was to get customers who already liked the fruit to buy more. Label design was used to promote oranges as a daily staple consumed for health, rather than a luxury fruit to be eaten on special occasions only.

Few people would sit and eat more than one orange at a time, but many people would squeeze and drink the juice of several oranges. The new labels emphasized orange juice for health. They suggested that people start the day with a glass of orange juice, and end it with an orange juice nightcap.

This campaign was aided considerably by the discovery of vitamins in 1915, and the realization of their necessity for a healthy life. The presence and importance of Vitamin C was used heavily in Sunkist advertising, including labels which showed healthy people consuming enticing glasses of orange juice. The effectiveness of the Sunkist Vitamin C campaign is that today we still consider oranges as the primary source of Vitamin C, rather than tomatoes or broccoli, which have equally high amounts.

A big campaign was undertaken to serve freshly squeezed orange juice at soda fountains. Special orange juice squeezers were developed for this use. During prohibition, hotel bars where orange juice was served were opened to women and children. *Corker* and *Extractor* were labels specifically aimed towards this market.

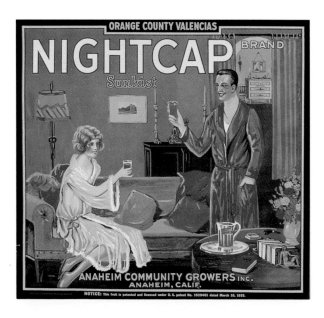

Women

The depiction of women on labels underwent a marked transition during the advertising age, starting with naturalistic portrait images, such as *Iva*, at the start of the 1920's, and going to representations of carefree young women like *California Eve* a few years later. *Seaside* and *Tropic*, reflecting the popularity of casual beach recreation and seaside vacations, are other new treatments from this period. *Treasure Chest* and *Tesero* show the influence of pin-up calendars published in the early 1930's by companies such as Brown and Bigelow.

A set of successful labels of attractive young women, including *Meritoria*, *Doria*, and *Favorita* was produced in the early 1920's from painted portraits by Duncan Gleason, a well known artist and illustrator of that era. Although the women on these labels appear different, all were painted from the same model, Gleason's future wife. In fact, they used the money from this commission to get married and take a honeymoon trip.

Another unusual feature of these particular labels is that the artist signed his works. Since the packer went to the trouble of commissioning the portraits through a major advertising agency and paid much more than normal for label art, he insisted that the artist's signature appear.

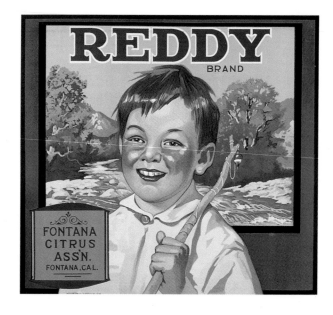

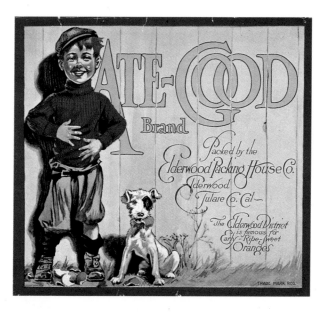

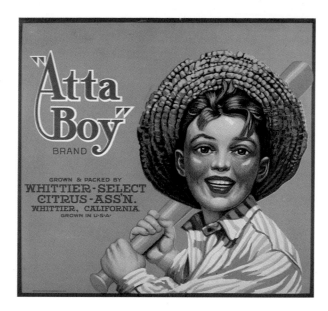

44

Children

American commercial illustrators have, over the years, used pictures of innocent and friendly children to represent a healthy, happy, and carefree life style. During the 1920's increasing numbers of orange growers chose label designs reflecting these themes.

Many growers pictured their own children or relatives. Although this carried on the older tradition of personal identification on labels, the design treatments were contemporary. Some brands, such as *Fontana Boy*, used a title which directly described the portrait. Others, like *Ate Good* and *Atta Boy*, combined unusual brand names with pictures less directly related to the title. *Ate-to-One* is a pun referring to the 8:1 ratio of sugar to acid in the ideal sweet orange; the picture of the enthusiastic lad helping himself to a box of oranges is only a loose association with the title.

Pasadena Luscious combines a young child with an attractively depicted partly peeled navel orange. This thick skinned orange is easy to peel and to divide into sections. It is so easy to prepare a child can do it.

O.C. is an effective advertising message. It shows a child and a box of oranges with the initial letters of the Orange Cove Citrus Association, a pun that calls attention to the high quality of the fruit.

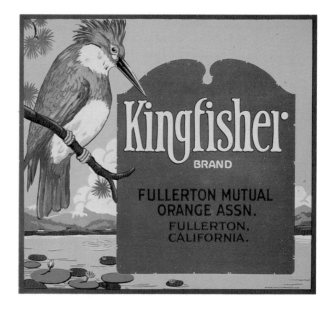

46

Birds and Animals

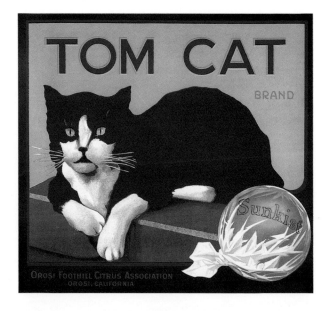

The depiction of birds and animals illustrates the wide variety of art styles used on labels in the 1920's. *Tom Cat* and *Kingfisher* show the flat color graphic poster style used on many outstanding labels of the period. *Cockatoo* represents the influence of decorative bird prints made by Jessie Arms Botke, among others. *Gosling* has a familiar cartoon-like look while *Fido* is a direct copy of the English comic character *Bonzo Dog*.

The changes in label design that took place during the advertising age can be quickly appreciated by comparing these labels with the earlier naturalistic treatments of similar subjects on pages 22-25. A definite attempt is made on the newer labels to establish a rapport with the customer. *Bunny* and *Tony,* in particular, communicate directly with the viewer in a friendly manner, compared to the more naturalistic *Jackrabbit* and *Nero.*

An increased emphasis on the quality of label lettering occurred at this time. The title provided label identification; it was important to integrate it with the label subject to form an effective advertisement.

Standard type was not used; letters were individually designed and arranged to complement the subject, forming a complete poster image.

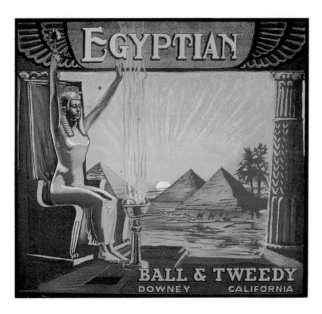

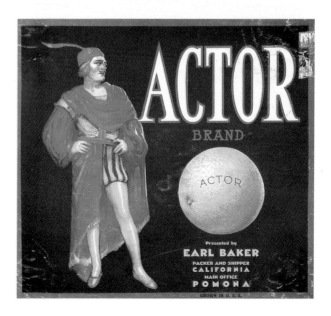

48

Entertainment

Movie stars and popular movie themes were depicted on a number of labels in the 1920's as movies made the transition from the nickelodeon one-reelers to music hall feature films.

Rudolph Valentino, the outstanding romantic hero of the decade, is shown on *Sheik* as a desert prince, and on *Don Juan* as a sophisticated Casanova, in a red-bordered frame. The depiction of cigarette smoking on orange labels shows the cultural changes that were underway in the 1920's.

Americans were fascinated with Arabian and Egyptian desert themes in the 1920's. While camels and pyramids had been favorite label subjects for years, the discovery and excavation of King Tut's tomb in 1922 and the widespread publicity it received added interested to this exotic subject. Egyptian themes appeared on a wide variety of decorative arts and advertisements, and were well represented on labels. *Egyptian* shows the new style of graphic design developing in this period.

Radio themes were not common on labels, but *Broadcast* conveys the impact of this dynamic new means of communication in a striking manner, and carries the new design spirit of the 1920's to the limit. The excitement and power of radio is emphasized by enclosing the scene in irregular borders and by using unusual color combinations.

Storybook Characters

Cartoon and storybook characters were adopted as trademark designs for many products during the 1920's. These included the Planter's Peanut man, the RCA Victor dog, the Cracker Jack sailor boy, and the Buster Brown boy with his dog. This success prompted many orange packers to try this form of product identification.

While many people in large cities were experiencing a new way of life during the "Roaring Twenties," a much more conservative life style prevailed in most rural areas where oranges were grown. Many of the growers were not at all attracted by the new flashy Art Deco labels, like the cigarette smoking *Don Juan*.

The more naive illustrations for children's books, which had gained a great deal of national attention during this period, provided alternative subjects for these growers. With the help of artists at Western Lithograph—the company that produced most of the labels with this type of subject—these packers received an attractive graphic image that was typically 1920's in design treatment.

For the most part, use of storybook characters as label subjects was confined to the 1920's. A few packers continued to use them, but the designs became oversimplified and uninteresting.

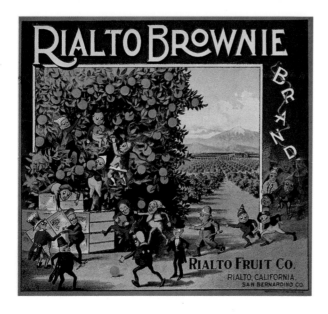

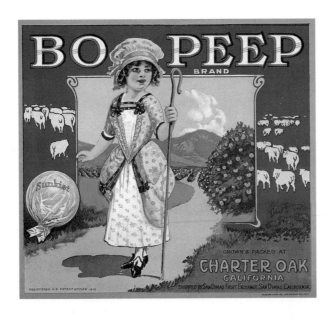

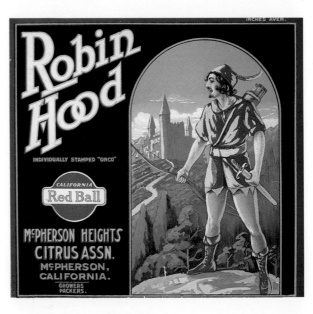

Stylized Images

Some of the new labels that emerged in this period reflected the "Art Deco" design movement. At its best, this art treatment created a feeling of modern elegance. On labels of the 1920's, it was combined with innovative color treatments, made possible because of the development of new printing ink formulations and sophisticated printing registration techniques. The result was a succession of attractive new label designs.

California Dream is a classic example, with its eye-catching design and complex but understated use of color. It also makes heavy use of bronzing, a technique where a gold layer is added to the design by selectively printing a layer of varnish on the label as a final printing step, and then dusting the label with a fine bronze powder that sticks to the still wet varnished areas. Bronzing was a slow and expensive additional step, seldom used to this extent on orange labels.

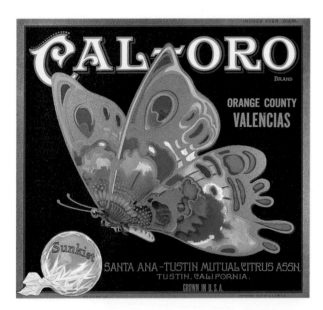

Cal-Oro carries the innovative use of color to an extreme; the flamboyant design is accented by placing it against a black background.

Flavorite successfully conveys its advertising message by using an unusual design theme and color treatment in conjunction with a prominent display of oranges as an integral part of the design.

Bold Poster Graphics

The 1920's were a time of experimentation and innovation in the label field, with the steady introduction of new label subjects, imaginative modernized treatments of older subjects, and the use of distinctive new design techniques. The concepts formulated by Don Francisco near the beginning of the decade for the development of successful labels were used more and more frequently.

Target, Celebration, and *Ace High* are classic examples of the new labels, with strong central images and label lettering well integrated into the general design. The graphic designs are clear and bold; the titles are concise and relevant.

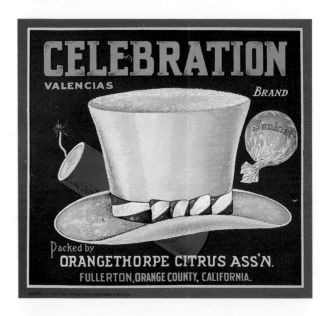

The treatment of the label as a small poster reached its peak with labels produced in this period. The ideas expressed by Charles Matlock Price in his book *The Poster* apply equally well to these successful orange box labels. "The poster must first catch the eye, and having caught it, hold the gaze, and invite further though brief inspection. The advertisement which is its reason for existence must be conveyed directly, clearly, and pictorially. It must be well designed, well colored, well printed, and well drawn—and these qualifications are stated in their order of importance."

CHAPTER III
COMMERCIAL ART (1935-1955)

By the mid 1930's over 35 million boxes of oranges were packed and shipped from California each year. The advertising campaigns of the 1920's had been effective; oranges had become a staple of the American diet. This large consumption required the production of more and more labels until the abrupt end of their use in the 1950's, when wooden boxes were replaced by cardboard boxes with preprinted images on their ends.

While large numbers of labels continued to be needed in the 1940's and 1950's, fewer and fewer new designs were introduced. Many older labels continued to be reprinted for years, sometimes with slight changes. Some in use in the 1930's had been essentially the same since the turn of the century.

Until the 1930's most label designers had traditional art training in Europe, or were taught by Europeans in American schools. After 1930, most aspiring designers were attending American commercial art schools where the focus was on product identification rather than aesthetic images. Label designs resulting from these new influences are in sharp contrast to the early naturalistic labels and to those of the 1920's.

The widespread use of photographic techniques for label production began in the 1930's. Instead of drawing the required set of color images on lithographic stones or metal plates, artists drew and colored a complete label on illustration board, and then transferred the design by photographic methods to a set of printing plates.

Since the artists were essentially painting pictures rather than producing sets of color separation images, they could use masking and taping procedures in conjunction with airbrush painting techniques, thus permitting the production of color gradation effects not possible with the older stippling processes. The *Circle* labels, designed in 1938, show the use of airbrush design.

Photographic techniques allowed artists to compose new labels and modernize older designs by superimposing sections of existing labels and by incorporating standard design elements. This greatly decreased design time and cost, and increased the flexibility of the design process.

Lower costs, made possible by photo-lithography and new design processes, were a necessity in the 1930's because of increased competitive pressure. The national economic depression had a severe effect on the citrus industry. This, of course, affected the price the packer was prepared to pay for his labels.

Competitive pressures were compounded by the arrival of printing companies

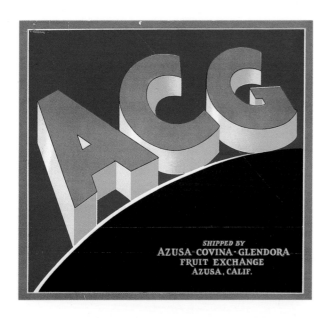

that had not been active in the citrus label field up to this time. In the search for new business, they produced inexpensive stock labels that could be used by anyone.

In spite of these problems, the overall quality of newly designed labels did not decrease during this period. The introduction of photolithography and new commercial design concepts prompted label artists to produce innovative high quality labels that effectively sold their product.

Block Letters and Geometric Images

Brand identification in the 1930's and 1940's often was emphasized by making three dimensional block letters the central subject. Visual impact was heightened by arranging the lettering in sloping or curved arrays, and by using airbrushed drop shadows.

Block letters had long been used in other aspects of commercial art, and in motion picture publicity and titles. It was difficult, though, to incorporate block letters with orange label subjects without having them conflict. Freedom to use lettering as the main image led to many new label treatments.

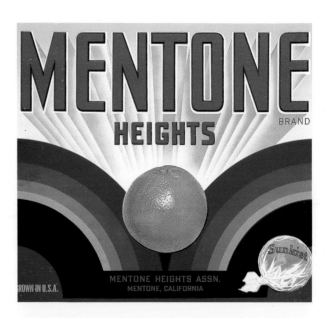

A wrapped orange was often included to increase product identification. Here, an integrated image was important, not merely the production of an attractive array of letters. While the orange in some cases looked like an incomplete afterthought, when well positioned it complimented the lettering.

Abstract geometric patterns, shown on many labels, were made more attractive by the subtle shading of airbrush techniques.

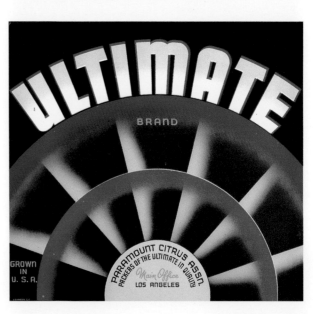

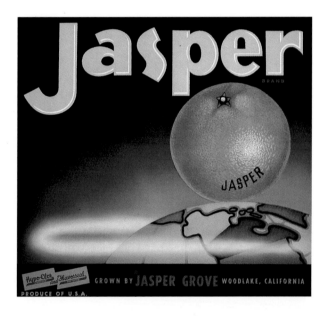

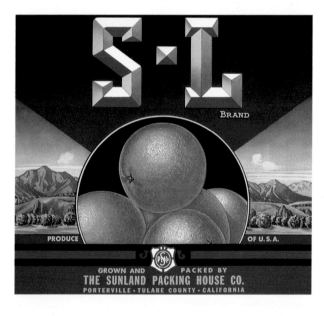

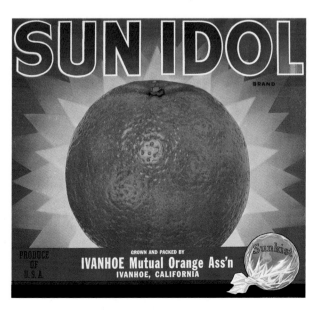

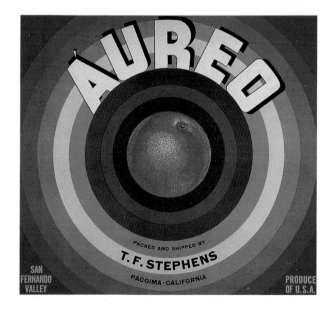

Oranges on Labels

Pictures of oranges were included on labels throughout the years. The fruit usually appeared as a standardized logo, or as part of a design where someone held an orange or drank a glass of orange juice. With increasing emphasis on product identification in the 1930's, oranges became more prominent and served as label subjects.

Since the design possibilities of using a large orange as the sole label subject were limited, it often was highlighted by surrounding it with colored circular rings, or placing it as the focal point of rainbows or sloping striped lines. A large orange sometimes was shown sitting on a mountain ridge, or as the sun sinking into the sea.

Large arrays of oranges were successfully used on labels. *Sanger Gold* and *Cascade O'Gold* give a dynamic feel to a subject that by nature is static.

The designer of *Million* took to heart the design rule that oranges should be prominently displayed on the label. More oranges are on this one label than many designers used in years of work.

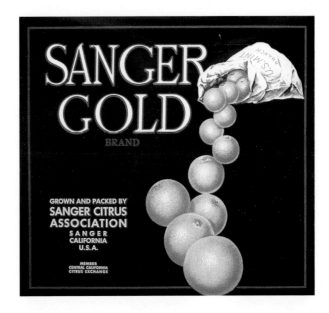

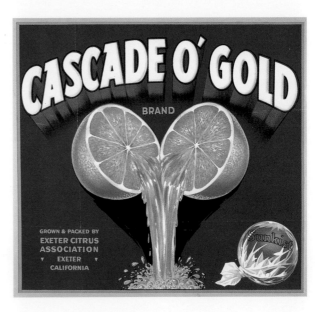

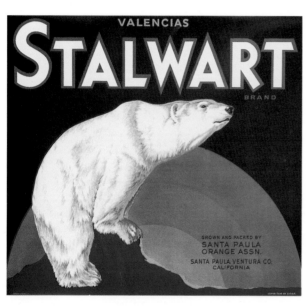

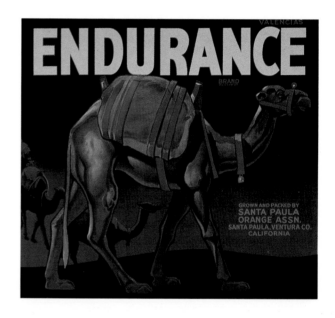

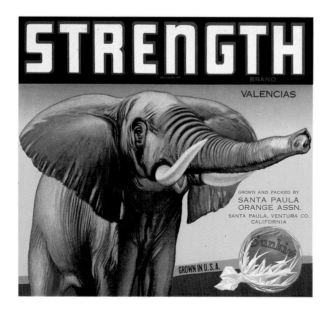

Animal and Cartoon Images

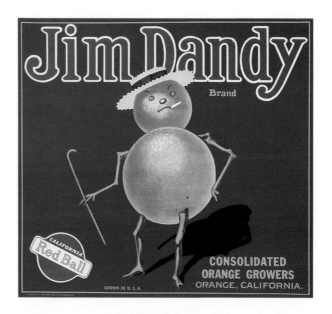

A notable series of labels designed by the Schmidt Lithograph Company for the Santa Paula Orange Association featured animals in interesting poses. Powerful titles were chosen to accompany these vigorous subjects, in order to create an optimistic feeling during the discouraging days of the depression.

Courage, with the lion emerging from the label toward the viewer, combined with jumbled lettering, is a far cry from the naturalistic lion of thirty or forty years earlier, as shown on *King* (page 25). The feeling of action and motion was rarely created as effectively. As with most labels featuring dynamic single images, the effect was multiplied when viewed as a series of images on a stacked array of boxes.

Out of Sight is the opposite extreme, a label that catches attention because of its incongruity and punning title.

Motion picture cartoons flourished in the 1930's. Humorous treatment of cartoon images presented sympathetic easily remembered images. *Jim Dandy, Half Moon* and *Anniversary* cleverly incorporate oranges and orange juice as design elements.

Women

Attractive women continued to be a favorite subject until the final days of label production. However, by the 1930's and 1940's the theme had been used so much that artists had difficulty in developing new design approaches.

By the mid 1930's photographs were replacing painted images in much commercial art and popular illustration. *Life* magazine, in particular, opened new horizons with its weekly treatment of news stories in photographic form.

While photographic treatment was a logical area for experimentation by label designers, the results in most cases were unsuccessful, since the design usually appeared static when photographs were combined with label lettering.

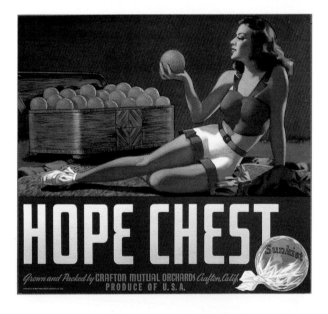

Label airbrush artists were so skilled at painting lifelike portraits and still life renderings of oranges that when presented with a choice, customers invariably chose the artist's renderings over photographic treatments. As a result, label artists continued to explore and improve the airbrush medium for several years after most commercial artists had abandoned the technique.

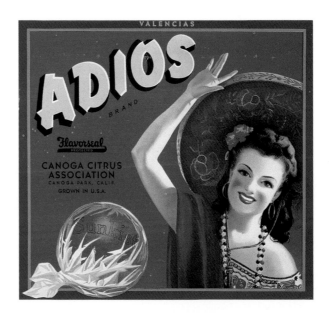

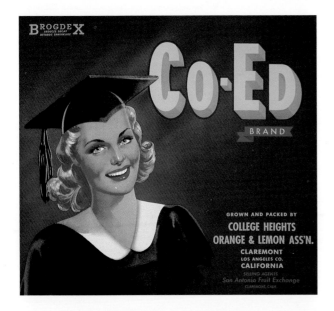

Late Labels

The depression period provided few new vigorous upbeat subjects for labels, compared to the 1920's emphasis on gaiety and zest for life, reflected on labels such as *Mirth* (page 37). The new San Francisco Golden Gate Bridge and Bay Bridge were two of the few contemporary images used as label subjects. *San Francisco* shows the Bay Bridge completed in 1936, which connected San Francisco with Oakland. The sharp modern image shows an impressive view of the San Francisco skyline.

Practically no labels were designed during World War II. Many younger artists were away at war, and the commercial art industry was busy with war related projects. However, a few labels were designed that dealt specifically with the war. *Convoy* and *Battlefield* are two members of a wartime series used by the Richgrove-Jasmine Citrus Association and the Sunflower Packing Corporation.

Few new labels were introduced in the postwar decade, the final ten years of label use. The citrus industry grew rapidly in this period, with marketing handled more and more by large organizations. The label's role as a personal tie between grower and consumer decreased. New labels often were bland simplified copies of earlier designs.

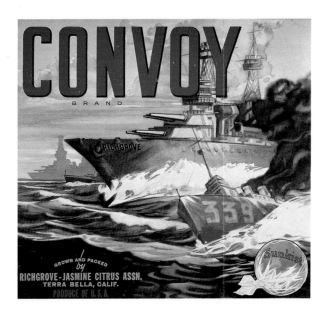

Cardboard Boxes

Major changes took place in the American marketing system in the late 1940's and early 1950's. The small grocery and produce stores of prewar years were replaced by supermarkets and shopping centers, as automobiles came into general use. The customer, with increased mobility, chose lower costs and greater product variety over personalized service.

Oranges were bought in large quantities by supermarkets who were less concerned with brand differences than the earlier jobbers and small fruit stores. Thus, the advertising value of the label became less important.

A rapid transition to new cardboard shipping containers occurred in the mid 1950's. They were labeled by printing the product identification directly on the cardboard stock before the box was assembled.

Since the label was used only for identification, designs became simplified, consisting of the brand name and a simple line drawing that usually was similar to the paper label it replaced. Most were printed in two colors only; green and orange or red and blue were popular combinations.

Although the new designs were simplified, many carried the general details of labels that had been used for decades. *Poppy* has the same design that was used in 1900 (page 26), and *Tesoro* and *Co-Ed* have the same general outline and lettering styles as their predecessors (pages 43 and 63).

Labels thus completed a seventy year journey ending in the 1950's as they had started in the 1880's, as simple identifications on the ends of boxes.

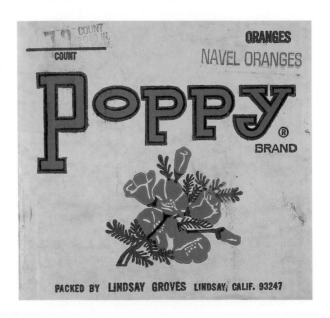

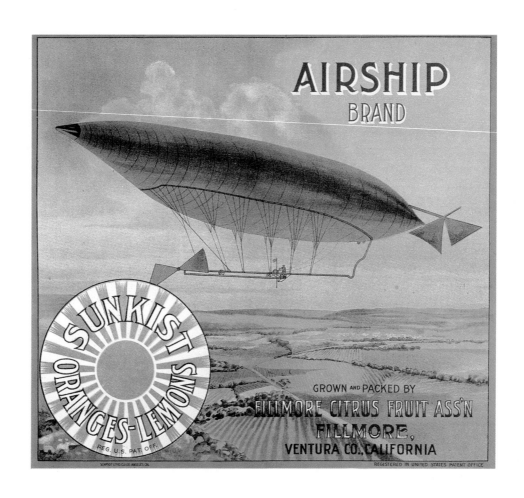

CHAPTER IV.
LABEL SUBJECTS

Labels have been discussed up to this point from a chronological point of view, illustrating changing design treatments, choice of subjects, and production techniques. This chapter will deal with a number of topics common to all periods of label use.

While many aspects of labels changed throughout their 70 year use, many stayed the same. Their size and general layout was the same in the 1950's as it had been in the 1890's. Advertising and product identification functions of the label continued throughout the period, although the relative emphasis of these roles changed. The label remained a quality product—great attention continued to be paid to label design and lettering, and no compromise was made in the quality of paper or printing methods.

While many subjects were more popular at some times than others, such as patriotic themes in the early days, storybook characters in the 1920's and block label subjects in the final period, certain subjects continued to be favorites. Women, Indians, Mexican themes, birds, flowers, animals and orchard scenes were used in large numbers for the entire period.

Art treatment slowly evolved from naturalism to impersonal stylized design. This reflected changes in commercial art design concepts, as well as the smaller role played by the grower in marketing and thus in label selection, as the industry grew.

In addition to their use on orange boxes, labels were used on other California citrus fruit. Grapefruit were shipped in the same size boxes as oranges, with similar labels. Lemons were shipped in a flatter box, with a label about 12″ x 9″. (See Hughes Transcontinental on page 127).

Many packinghouses shipped lemons or grapefruit in addition to oranges, and often used the same label titles and subjects, changing the design slightly in the case of lemons to take the different label dimensions into account. Some special subjects were often used—desert scenes on grapefruit labels, and seacoast scenes on lemon labels.

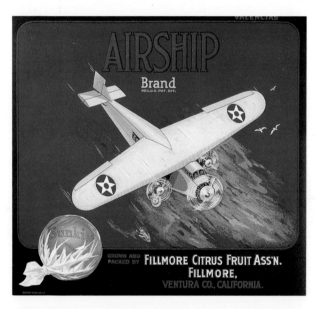

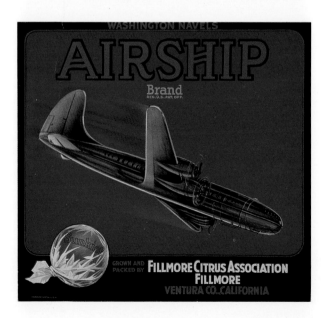

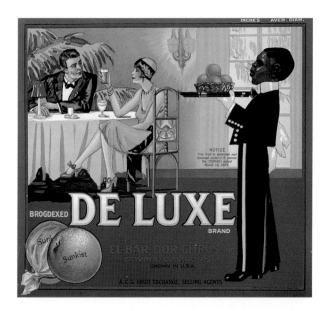

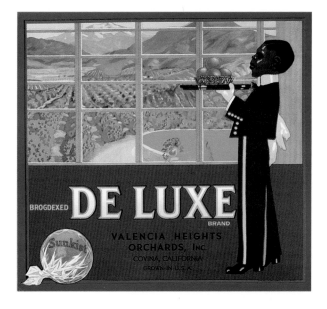

Label Evolution

Most successful label designs were used for years and redesigned only when they were clearly old fashioned, or when a new design decision was precipitated by a change of label printer or by a change in ownership of the packing association. New labels and label concepts slowly were added, and outmoded topics slowly were phased out. Label titles rather than label subjects usually were registered or copyrighted; when fruit growers associations and packinghouses were reorganized, the titles passed to new owners.

Many labels continued to be used for long periods with the same title, with evolving subject treatment. *Airship* was used for 60 years, but since the subject was one that quickly became outmoded, the design was steadily updated. *De Luxe* kept the same image of the black waiter, while going from a 1918 restaurant scene, to a 1920's pseudo-speakeasy and finally, to a 1930's orchard. Hundreds of similar examples of updated labels could be given.

To show how labels changed while staying the same in general characteristics, three pairs of labels are shown—the version in use before the 1920's and the one in use in 1950. While the older versions can easily be distinguished from the newer ones, the general design features remain the same.

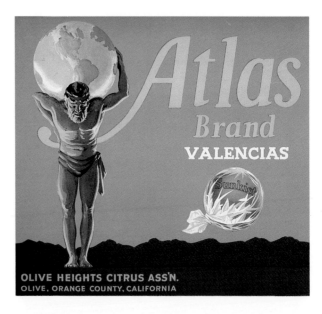

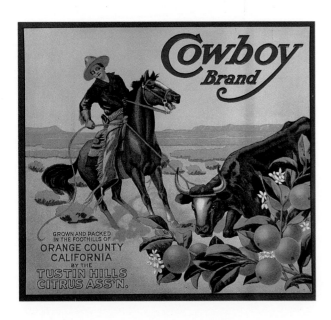

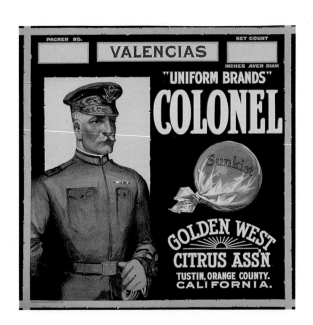

PACKER NO.   VALENCIAS   NET COUNT

INCHES AVER DIAM

"UNIFORM BRANDS"
COLONEL

Sunkist

GOLDEN WEST
CITRUS ASS'N.
TUSTIN, ORANGE COUNTY.
CALIFORNIA.

GREEN HUSSAR

ALTA LOMA
HEIGHTS
CITRUS ASSN

ALTA LOMA
CALIFORNIA

PACKER NO.   VALENCIAS   NET COUNT

INCHES AVER. DIAM.

"UNIFORM BRANDS"
CAPTAIN

CALIFORNIA
Red Ball

GOLDEN WEST
CITRUS ASS'N.
TUSTIN, ORANGE COUNTY
CALIFORNIA

RED HUSSAR

ALTA LOMA
HEIGHTS
CITRUS ASS'N.

CALIFORNIA
Red Ball

ALTA LOMA
CALIFORNIA

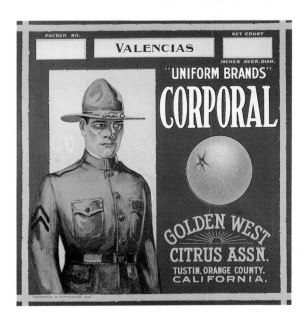

PACKER NO.   VALENCIAS   NET COUNT

INCHES AVER. DIAM.

"UNIFORM BRANDS"
CORPORAL

GOLDEN WEST
CITRUS ASS'N.
TUSTIN, ORANGE COUNTY.
CALIFORNIA.

BLUE HUSSAR

Sunkist

ALTA LOMA
HEIGHTS
CITRUS ASSN.

ALTA LOMA
CALIFORNIA

Sets of Labels

Orange growers and packers faced the problem that, while oranges in any given crop were of varying quality and size, the entire output had to be sold. Nearly all producers packed and shipped at least three grades of fruit, each with a separate label. The quality of fruit was identified in a way well known to the produce middlemen, but not immediately obvious to a customer buying one of the secondary grades.

Members of the California Fruit Growers Association used the *Sunkist* trademark on the top grade, *Red Ball* on the intermediate grade and an unmarked orange, or no product identification at all, on the lowest grades. A color code was sometimes used, with blue being the highest grade, red the intermediate, and green the lowest.

The Golden West Citrus Association "Uniform Brands" made the quality distinction by both Sunkist trademarks and military ranks. The Alta Loma Heights Citrus Association set made the distinction by color, also used on *Circle* (page 55). The Yorba Orange Growers *King David* set made the subtle ranking distinction by status. This, incidentally, is one of the rare examples of biblical themes on orange labels.

Other examples of quality sets are the *Diplomat* series consisting of *Ambassador, Diplomat, Envoy* and *Consul*; and, the *Chess* series of *King, Queen, Bishop, Knight* and *Rook*.

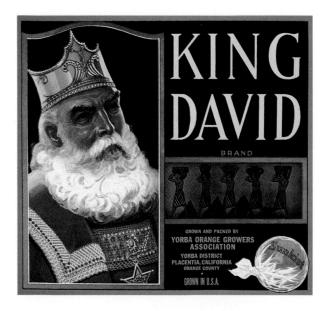

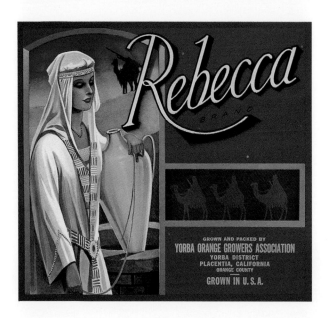

71

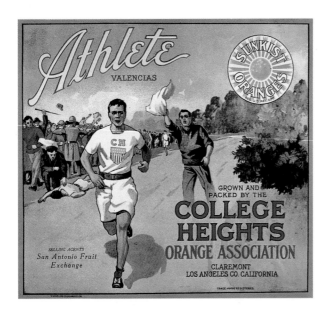

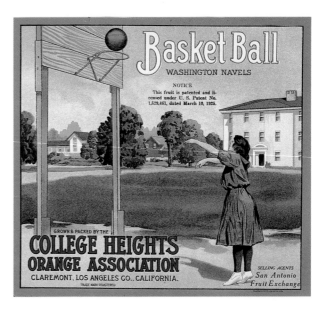

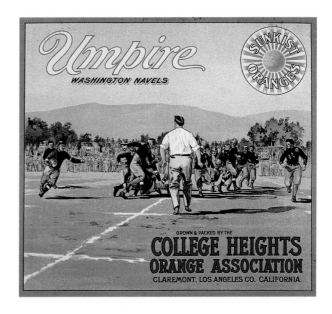

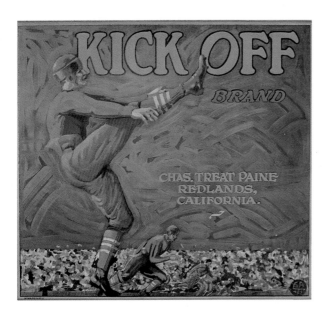

Sports

Relatively few sports scenes were depicted on labels, considering the widespread American interest in athletics throughout the years. During the period when labels were used, baseball was the only popular professional sport; the others were amateur or collegiate activities.

Baseball, football, basketball, track and golf were treated on early labels, along with outdoor activities such as skiing and bike riding. It was not easy to develop modifications of these subjects, or additions to the obvious label titles.

An additional problem that restricted the use of sports themes on labels was that most dramatic sports scenes show group activity, which did not lend itself to the single central image design treatment on successful posters.

The key user of sports subjects was the College Heights Orange Association, which first employed them in the early 1900's, and then continued to modernize and update the designs. A later version of *Athlete* is shown on page 99.

Cycle underwent an interesting evolution. Starting as a bicyclist on the 1890's label, it soon featured a motorcyclist and finally, with a complete change of design theme, a set of circles labeled spring, summer, fall and winter.

PACKED BY
TUSTIN PACKING CO.
E.E.WILSON.
AGENT.
ORANGE, CAL.
TUSTIN, CALIFORNIA.

CUCAMONGA CITRUS FRUIT GROWERS ASSN.
CUCAMONGA, CAL.
SELLING AGENTS
O.K. FRUIT EXCHANGE UPLAND CAL.

HEWES' TRANSCONTINENTAL BRAND

GROWN AND PACKED BY
D. HEWES
EL MODENA
HIGHLANDS
ORANGE, CAL.
GROWN IN ABSOLUTELY FROSTLESS BELT.

Transportation

America's growth was due to expanded means of transportation. Immigrants came to America by ship and crossed the country by railroad. The automobile changed the economic and social structure of the entire population.

Development of the orange industry became possible because railroads linked Southern California to the east. Trainloads of fruit were shown on many early labels, as on *Riverside* (page 4) and *Hewes Transcontinental*. David Hewes, a successful San Francisco businessman and Southern California citrus grower, had a special interest in trains, having helped drive the golden spike that completed the Central Pacific Railroad. On later labels, trains were shown in dramatic scenes like *Flyer*, rushing fruit to market.

Sailing ships were popular subjects throughout the years, with colorful billowing sails providing attractive label compositions. In the early 1900's, the years following the Spanish-American War and the development of America's international military presence, United States Navy ships often were shown.

Automobiles seldom appeared as central images on labels, *Auto* being a notable exception. But, they often were shown in orchard or scenic surroundings as in the 1900's *Sunshine Grove* (page 9), the 1920's *National Park* and *Yorba Linda Gem* (page 37) and the 1930's *Highway* (page 96).

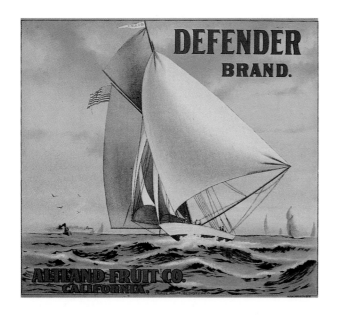

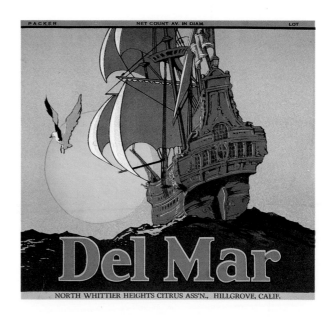

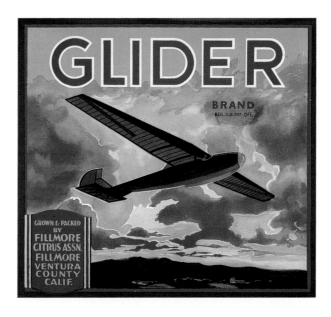

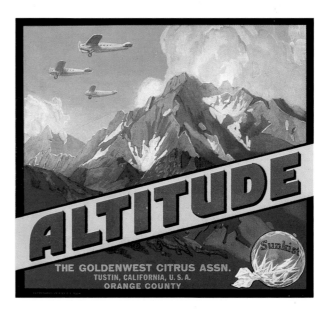

Airplanes

The use of orange box labels paralleled the development of the airplane. The first labels were produced when tentative aerial experiments were taking place, leading to the first manned flights in the early 1900's; the final labels were produced as passenger jets became a reality. The development of the airplane was steadily chronicled on labels.

The best known depiction was the Fillmore Citrus Association *Airship* series (pages 66-67). It began in the 1890's with a Jules Verne-like one-man dirigible, followed by steadily updated designs featuring military aircraft. The final one showed a futuristic four engine passenger airplane, designed several years before such planes became a reality.

The Golden West Citrus Association chose an airplane theme when it replaced its "Uniform" series with a more modern subject. The California aircraft industry developed in Orange County near the Golden West groves, so this was a natural choice. *Top Flight* shows a famous airplane of the 1930's, the transpacific China Clipper.

While airplanes on labels often were lost in background scenery, the careful positioning and use of dramatic clouds make *Glider* a successful design.

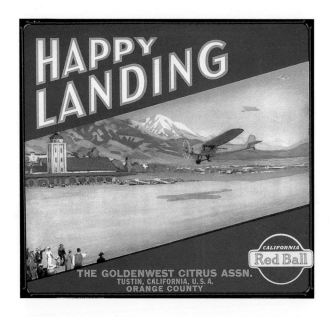

Large Images

Since the purpose of the orange box label was to identify and advertise the contents, a large orange was a natural subject.

Three examples of turn of the century treatment of oranges are shown here. Incongruously large oranges are shown with Palmer Cox brownies, with an elephant, and with a fetching young girl in a white dress. The depiction of oversized fruit and vegetables was a favorite humorous theme on postcards and trade cards of the period. Images such as a single large orange filling a railroad car and drawings of large vegetables in human form were common.

As the years passed, a number of less interesting labels were designed, showing a single large orange with lettering superimposed in front. *Flavorite* (page 52), a 1920's label with butterfly-winged fairies and large oranges, was a welcome exception.

In the 1930's and 1940's, with emphasis on lettering and product identification, the subject became reinvigorated. *Egnaro* (page 86) combining an orange with block lettering, is a successful composition, the curved lettering giving a three dimensional appearance to the orange. Other labels of the period show innovative treatments of the subject (pages 58-59).

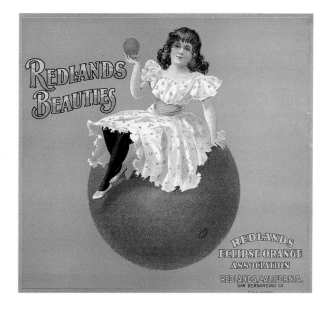

Large Letters

Because wholesale purchasers viewed orange boxes from about 10 feet away, it was important to design the label for maximum impact at that distance, according to Don Francisco's design suggestions.

A number of orange growers heeded this advice. They wanted a direct identification with their packing house, and so used a large single letter as the central subject, often the initial letter of their packing association, such as *Big R* for the Rialto Orange-Lemon Association and *Red C* for the Covina Citrus Association. Or, they used the initial letter of the town in which they were located, as in *Big U* for the Old Baldy Citrus Association of Upland.

Early labels using this treatment had flat letters, in circles or ovals. Later labels, especially when new commercial design concepts were used, made effective designs with large single block letters, creating a three-dimensional appearance.

Big R underwent a steady evolution, starting with the giant flat R superimposed on an orchard scene shown here, and going to an even larger block R with the letter hooking to the bottom of the label. The final version became simplified, with a Gothic script R on a plain brown background.

Big U showed a large orange in the loop in the U. Whatever one thinks of its design merits, this label certainly identified the product and could be seen easily from a distance.

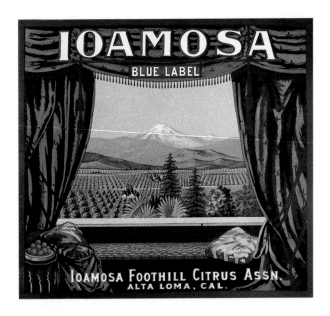

80

Framed Images

The most common label design throughout the years showed a citrus orchard with snow covered mountains in the background.

This pleasant image well described the geographical area where the orange groves were located. However, overuse made it boring and ineffective, not suitable for distinct product identification.

This problem was solved on some labels by enclosing the scene in a frame or between curtains. This permitted the use of a foreground person or object to provide a focal point, while still keeping the pleasant association of Southern California scenery. The label viewer shares the scene with the person in the foreground.

Sierra Vista Rancho is especially well thought out, since the dog seems to be completely outside the label, looking in.

Honora is a classic label, with both an interesting foreground and background, and a strong feeling of depth.

Wonder carries the framing technique one step further, putting the orange on a stage framed by curtains and pillars. The use of lighting and shading calls special attention to the wrapped fruit.

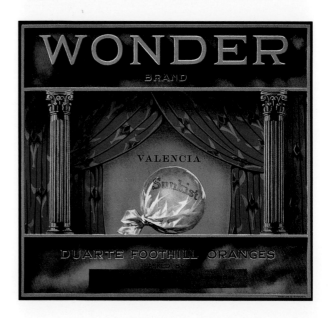

Blacks

While black people were extremely popular subjects in 19th and early 20th century advertisements and labels, they appeared on a relatively small number of orange box labels. These stereotyped depictions are rightfully considered offensive today, but at the time they were standard themes on trade cards, sheet music, postcards, and advertisements.

Blacks in fancy regalia were used regularly on theater, minstrel show, and vaudeville posters. *Red Rover,* with his long red coat and diamond stickpin, was designed by the McLaughlin Brothers in New York, who also used the design as a cover illustration on one of their game boards.

A number of labels showed blacks as waiters, as in *Porter* and the *De Luxe* series, balancing trays of oranges.

Topsy was part of a cartoon series designed in the 1930's, guaranteed to offend anyone who took the labels at all seriously. Other members of the set were *Buckaroo,* showing a slack-jawed cowboy on a miniature horse and *Old Rip,* a yawning old man with a straggly long white beard, tattered clothes, and holes in his shoes.

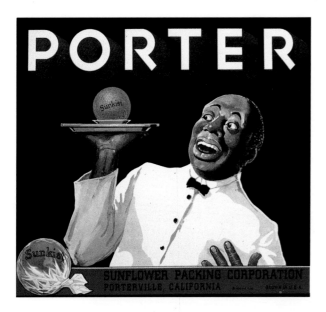

Export Labels

There is a large export market for California oranges, especially in the Orient, Australia, and New Zealand, where there is little competition with fruit from Europe and Africa.

Most export oranges were shipped with the same labels used in the United States. A few organizations with large foreign trade, such as Getz Brothers and the Australian New Zealand American Trading Company (Anaco) in San Francisco designed a number of special labels for foreign sales.

A few labels aimed for the Chinese market had titles and advertising messages in Chinese. The *Charles N. Kim* label discusses how sweet and delicious his oranges are, that the quality is high and the price is reasonable. Kim says that he appreciates his Chinese customers and will cheat neither young or old. He states "It is the very best thing to give oranges as a gift".

Nine Sons appeals to Chinese patriotism in the 1920's, showing the nationalist Chinese flag and portraits of martyrs from the Chinese Revolution of 1911.

The *Slowe & Co.* label, designed specifically for the Shanghai trade, gives the name of the Shun Fa (prosperity) market.

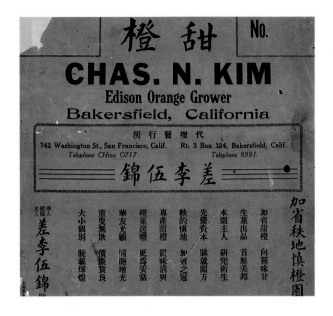

Label Variations

Stock labels were used steadily in large quantities as inexpensive ways of labeling orange boxes, dealing with fruit of low quality, or shipping special small quantities. The minimum run for standard labels was usually 25,000. If fewer were needed, or if special labels were needed in a hurry, a stock label with a letterpress title could be used.

The *Mountain High* stock label with an attractive well framed image was popular. It survives with combinations of over a dozen different titles and packers.

The *Yacht* series shows the complex boundary between stock labels and custom labels. Six distinct labels are shown—far from the complete number in the series—for six different packers, with four different design variations and five titles. It probably started as a stock label and proved so popular it was redesigned on several occasions as a custom label.

Labels such as these complicate the matter of determining how many different label designs were produced. The number of distinct designs, at least 8000, easily can be doubled if slight variations, as shown here, are included and if special additional lettering is taken into account.

Coined Words

An interesting group of labels are those whose titles are artificially coined words, using puns, novel spelling, or letter reversal. The results, as is the case with any word manipulation ranged from being very clever to tedious and ponderous.

Ak-Sar-Ben was one of the earliest uses of a play on words. The first label using this title (Nebraska spelled backwards) showed portraits of the Marks brothers in turn-of-the-century photographs. The title was used on a succession of labels for half a century.

Egnaro, with the large orange emphasizing block lettering, is another example of letter reversal. *Cali-4-nia* used novel spelling to make a title that would be remembered. *O.C* (page 45) used a punning title to call attention to the high quality of the fruit.

As the years passed, coined words were used more and more often. This was done partly as a desire for originality, but also because so many thousands of titles were already in use that the discovery of an innovative new one became increasingly difficult. It must have been discouraging for a shipper looking over a list of registered label titles, to find that even *Dry Bog* and *Saw Tooth* had been used.

Blemished Fruit

One problem faced by orange growers was that fruit of good quality often had an unattractive external appearance. Oranges sometimes had surface blemishes or discoloration, which had no effect on their taste or quality of the juice. Also, Valencia oranges tended to lose their bright orange color and become greenish again near the end of the growing season when the nights became cooler. These were difficult to sell.

Several labels were developed to emphasize the good quality of the fruit and juice inside the rough exterior.

Golden Surprise illustrates this message in obvious terms, with the Indian's expression changing from disgust to delight as he views the opened orange. *Camouflage* does not feel it wise to display the fruit itself and uses the message "The quality is inside." Other labels of this sort are *Hobo,* with the slogan "Beauty is but skin deep—not so bad as they look," and *Peasant* showing an unattractive wrinkled lady saying "Sweeter than I look."

Mutt uses a popular comic strip character of the 1930's and 1940's from Bud Fisher's Mutt and Jeff. The colorful label points out the positive aspects of the fruit—"Not so much for looks but sweet, ripe, and juicy."

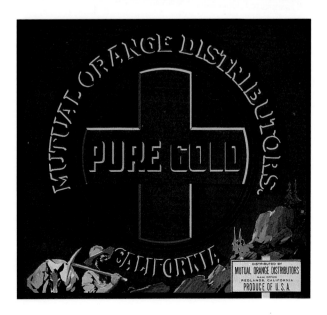

Marketing Organizations

The early orange growers realized that they needed cooperative marketing activities to successfully sell their products in Eastern markets. After the failure of a number of early organizations due to poor control of the marketing process, the California Fruit Growers Exchange was formed in 1906. It attracted a large number of California growers, and grew rapidly and steadily, until by the 1930's it marketed over 75% of the California crop.

The CFGE realized the need for consistent product identification and for large scale advertising campaigns. It developed the Sunkist trademark and logo for the premium product in 1908; in 1911 the Red Ball designation was given to the second quality fruit. The first Sunkist logo was the Sunburst design, as shown on Airship (page 66). After several redesigns, the wrapped orange logo shown here was used.

Growers who were members of the CFGE in general kept their own brand identity, incorporating the various logos on their regular labels. The *Sunkist* and *Red Ball* labels shown here were used for products shipped directly by the CFGE, often for export sales.

An auxiliary organization, The Fruit Growers Supply Company, was set up to supply various products including labels for members of the CFGE. It consolidated label purchases, and put the label requirements for members of the exchange out for annual bid.

A second large cooperative, the Mutual Orange Distributors, was formed in 1908. Organized along the same general lines as the CFGE, it used Pure Gold and Silver Seal as designations for the top two grades. Many members of the organization used standard labels for their shipments, the *Sunflower, Goldenrod, Poppy,* and *Pansy* brands.

In 1918 a third national marketing organization, the American Fruit Growers, began to sell California citrus fruit. This nationwide organization marketed a wide variety of fruits and vegetables, from Maine potatoes and Washington apples to California and Florida oranges. Their *Blue Goose* logo was the most widely recognized trademark ever designed for agricultural products.

As California growers began to have their oranges marketed by the American Fruit Growers, they made a transition from the labels they had been using by incorporating the Blue Goose logo on their labels, as on *Summer Girl,* or by including a small version of their label on the standard Blue Goose label.

Another distinctive feature of the American Fruit Growers labels was the use of two color printing, blue and orange. This was used for all the Blue Goose labels, as well as for special labels such as *Mustang.* All the labels used by the American Fruit Growers were lithographed by Western Lithograph in Los Angeles.

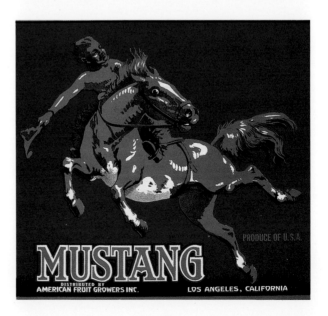

Western Scenery

In addition to the orchard and snow capped mountain theme that appeared on large numbers of labels throughout the years, the mountains, canyons, rivers and lakes of the West were favorite subjects.

The natural beauty of Yosemite National Park was steadily shown. In the early labels, scenes are naturalistic and true to life, showing the sheer cliffs of *El Capitan, Half Dome,* and *Sentinel Rock. Big Tree* shows the famous large redwood, with a tunnel in the base large enough to drive a carriage through. Yosemite scenes continued to be label favorites, with less realistic depictions as the years passed.

Geyser shows Old Faithful in Yellowstone National Park, *Grand Canyon,* a sunrise scene with an interesting foreground silhouette.

These labels, along with *National Park* (page 37) achieved a design treatment worthy of high quality travel posters.

Western scenery was a favorite label subject as long as labels were used, although in later years the design became more general and abstract, and locations and titles of specific scenes were used less often.

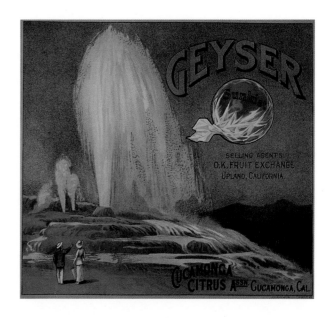

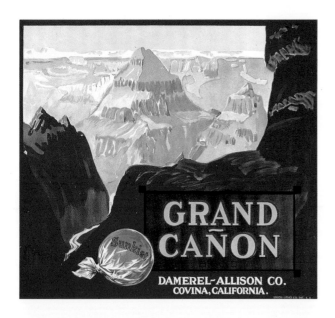

Brino College of Lithography—1929

CHAPTER V.
LABEL ARTISTS

Orange box labels were designed mainly by artists working for California lithographers. These firms did a wide variety of commercial art work—advertisements, posters, showcards, stock certificates and business forms. While they produced thousands of box labels, it was still only a small part of their business.

The art departments in these firms usually were small—an art director and a few artists. The art director, in addition to supervising the in-house art staff, commissioned free-lance artists to design additional labels to meet customer requirements during busy periods.

Label design was a high pressure job. Staff artists were expected to work hard and produce quality work quickly. Consequently, there was a high turnover among lithograph house artists. Many became free-lance artists or switched firms often. Art directors, on the other hand, usually held well paid secure positions and tended to work for many years for the same company.

As is the case with most commercial art, few artists were allowed to sign their designs. Due to the changing composition of art staffs, owners did not want to have work associated with specific artists. Also, most labels were not designed by one artist. Usually, one did the pictorial illustration and another produced the lettering. The concept of two artists working on the same label became a very successful way to produce high quality designs in a relatively short time, and was used for the entire 70 year period of label production.

Many lettering and script specialists, particularly those working from the turn of the century until the 1930's, were well paid and treated with great respect. Lithography firms needed them also to design and engrave the elaborate letterheads, stock certificates and documents that were an important part of their business. This work was done in soundproof rooms where everyone breathed in a way so as not to break the silence, until the department head softly signaled for a rest period. These artists in many cases worked under magnifying glasses to achieve the fine detail required. Those with enough ability to do this type of work and the patience to concentrate for extended periods were hard to find, valued employees.

One such person was Armin Tesch. His exceptionally fine script lettering style made him nationally famous within the trade during the 1890's and the early 1900's. He was in such demand that lithograph companies all over the country paid his way to work at their plants on special projects. About 1906 he settled in Los Angeles and began working for the Western Lithograph Company. He was responsible for designing some of the finest lettering on Western's labels, stock certificates and letterheads before he retired in the 1930's.

Illustrators in this pre-1930's period worked somewhat differently than the lettering artists. First they made a watercolor sketch of the basic label design for the customer to see. Once the sketch was approved the artist, or sometimes a separate engraver, mentally worked out the color separations and drew the correct images on several different stone or aluminum plates, which when inked and fed through the press accurately recreated the original sketch.

This type of work required skilled artists who trained for many years to perfect their art styles. Many were European immigrants who had studied and worked in the lithographic trade before moving to California, experience that helped them to immediately get work when they arrived. Their enthusiasm for the paradise they found in California is reflected in their pictorial label designs.

By the late 1920's it became clear that major technical changes were beginning to occur. Photographic processes were completely changing the way pre-production label art was done. Illustrations and lettering were painted on high quality art board and photographically transferred to lithograph plates.

These changes, combined with the fact that older artists, some of whom had been working for the companies since the turn of the century and now were about to retire, forced the lithograph companies to take action. Replacing these men with competent employees who knew the trade and could produce quality work was difficult.

To resolve this problem the lithographers joined together and formed an organization called the Color Association, which in turn subsidized an art school in San Francisco to teach promising young students. Each lithograph company sponsored one or two students. When training was complete the artist worked for an agreed number of years at the company that sponsored him. The school was officially known as the Brino College of Lithography, but was commonly known as "Brino's School," after the head instructor Ambrose J. Breininger.

Mr. Breininger had studied art and learned the lithography trade in England before moving to San Francisco. There he became an active artist, art collector, teacher and member of the Bohemian Club. He taught students at the school virtually every aspect of the business including how to produce art on lithograph stones, metal plates and art boards; the entire lithograph process up to and including proof reading of printed sheets; and, practical details of the photographic processes they would be using. Students were given actual jobs from the lithographic firms, which they completed under the teacher's supervision.

Graduates from "Brino's School," along with other trained graphic artists of this time, were responsible for the new style of label design. They were very aware of current trends in poster graphics, magazine illustrations, and other popular commercial designs. Trade magazines and newsstand publications were full of color illustrations by the world's leading commercial artists. These images had a great deal of influence on the way labels were beginning to be designed.

Undoubtedly, the most influencial magazine advertisements were those produced or supervised by Charles Everett Johnson. A native California born in Gilroy

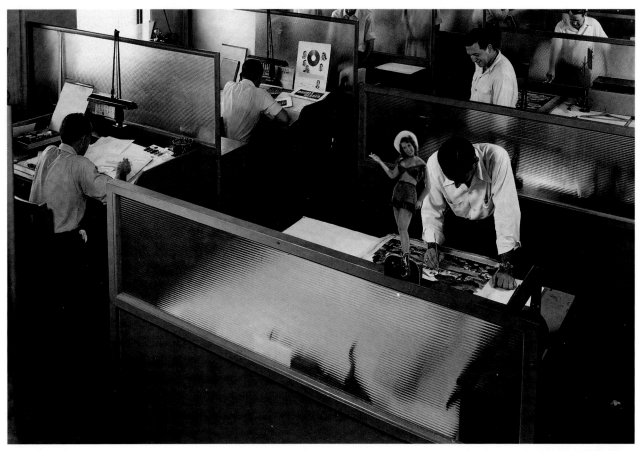

Western Lithograph

in 1866, Johnson received his formal art education in Paris with Richard Miller, and at the Chicago Art Institute.

In 1913, while working as art director for the Lord and Thomas Advertising Agency, he was put in charge of the Sunkist account. Within a few years this advertising campaign was a national success. From the 1920's to the 1940's he operated a freelance studio in Los Angeles, where he produced many paintings which first appeared as Sunkist magazine ads and then became label images. *Sunny Cove* is an example of the style he was known for. In addition, he hired other well known and up and coming artists to design advertisements. One was Duncan Gleason, who produced the illustration of the young woman for the *Sonia* label. Three additional labels and more information about Gleason can be found on page 42.

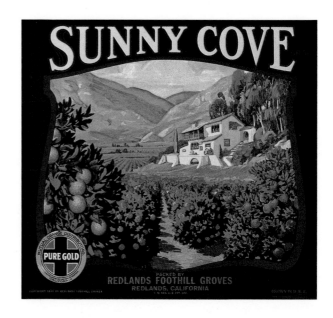

Other prominent California artists who participated in designing Sunkist advertising and/or labels were Andrew Loomis, known for his Coca Cola tray illustrations of the 1920's and 1930's; Maurice Logan, a founding partner of the Logan, Cox and Carey advertising firm in San Francisco and well known in the Bay area as a fine artist; Sam Hyde Harris, an award winning poster artist and easel painter in Los Angeles; Earl Cordery, a nationally recognized illustrator for Colliers magazine; Jimmy Swinnerton, the producer of a well known comic strip; and, the famous western artist Frank Tenny Johnson. Western Lithograph Company had a contract with Johnson which gave the firm exclusive rights to reproduce his paintings as calendar prints and occasionally as label designs. *Summit* was a typical Johnson illustration.

On the following pages are biographical sketches of other artists that produced label designs, along with illustrations of labels that are attributed to them.

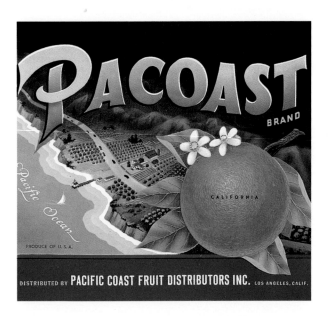

Adrian Apple

Adrian Apple attended high school and art classes in Cleveland, Ohio. After serving in World War I he came to California and settled in Los Angeles. His first job was with the Neuner Lithograph Company, where he began designing fruit box labels. From 1925-1933 he operated a freelance commercial art studio in Glendale. His many commissions included greeting card designs, book illustrations, magazine and newspaper advertisements, as well as labels. Much of his work came to him through advertising agencies and art directors at various lithographic companies.

In 1933 he began designing labels for the Western Lithograph Company and continued to work for them off and on until his retirement in the early 1950's. Most of his label art was done with an air brush and stencils. He specialized in bold, modern lettering. *Pacoast*, *Highway*, and *Stardust* are examples of the work he produced during the 1933-1950 period.

Sidney Armer

Sidney Armer was born in San Francisco in 1871 and lived there until the 1950's. After working as a designer at the Dickman-Jones Company in the 1890's, he became a freelance artist, specializing in illustrations of California plants and flowers. His watercolor sketches were purchased by various lithograph companies who used them as extremely accurate illustrations on fruit box labels. The Traung Label and Lithograph Company in particular used many of his botanical studies on the labels they produced in the 1920's.

Ralph Baker

After high school Ralph Baker attended "Brino's School" in San Francisco in the late 1920's. Upon graduation he worked for the Taung Label and Lithograph Company as a full time label artist. He worked there from 1930 to 1970, as the firm underwent several mergers. For several years after Othello Michetti retired in the 1960's, Baker was the art director for Stecher, Traung, and Schmidt. *Chalet* is an example of his commercial art.

C.A. Beck

C.A. Beck worked full time as a label and poster designer from about 1900 until the 1930's. He lived in Burlingame, south of San Francisco, where he had a unique home filled with paintings and three dimensional objects he produced in his spare time.

Before the 1906 earthquake he was a staff artist at Mutual Label and Lithograph Company, where he designed a number of successful stock label images. He also is credited with creating many of the original versions of classic turn-of-the-century custom label designs. Later he worked at the Schmidt Lithograph Company where he and Henry Gorham directed a number of staff artists as well as freelance artists contracted to handle the overflow. For the most part he did watercolor sketches and illustrations of still life subjects and human figures. Occasionally he went on location to paint landscapes and views of citrus groves.

During the first half of this century Schmidt Lithograph produced many thousands of different citrus label designs. Mr. Beck was directly responsible for many

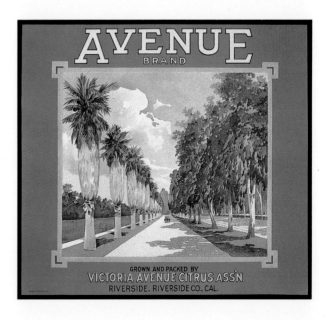

of these. He was certainly one of the most important figures in the field of label art.

His work spanned the transition from stone lithography to offset printing and photocomposition techniques. *Royal* is a turn of the century design, *Avenue* a classic example from the 1920's, and *Mansion* a label from the early 1930's.

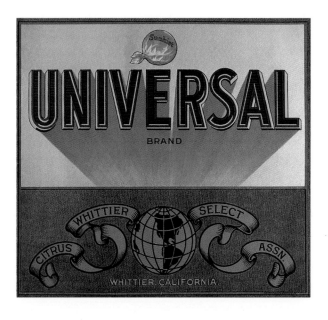

Bissiri Studios

Two brothers, Augusto and Adriano Bissiri, opened a commercial art studio in Los Angeles about 1915. They were immigrants from Seui, Sardinia and had studied art before coming to California. They specialized in lettering and worked regularly for Western Lithograph from the 1920's to the 1950's designing labels and doing special lettering jobs. They also were well known for producing titles for motion pictures for all the major studios. *Universal* is typical of their work.

Al Clark

Al was the youngest of the three Clark brothers who came to San Francisco from Bristol, England. After attending "Brino's School" he went to work for Western Lithograph for one year. From 1934 to the mid-1950's he operated a freelance studio in San Francisco and designed many labels, including *Vandalia*. He worked almost exclusively with an air brush and did both lettering and illustration.

Ted Clark

Ted Clark came to San Francisco in 1922 at the age of 18 and got a full time job as a label designer for the Traung Label and Lithograph Company. Much of his actual art education was on-the-job training with art director Othello Michetti. He learned to work quickly and skillfully with watercolors and tempera paints on art board, using both brushes and airbrush techniques.

In 1933 when business at Traung became slow he and his brother Al opened a freelance studio in San Francisco, where they produced art for most of the label lithographers in both San Francisco and Los Angeles. From 1936 until the mid 1960's he was the art director for the Carton Label Company in San Francisco, which later was owned by the Security Lithograph Company, and then Diamond International. When he took over the art department at Carton Label he was the only staff artist and was given the job of designing and redesigning hundreds of orange box labels; this was his full time job for several years.

The three examples here represent the different types of jobs he worked on. *Orbit* was one of his original designs. *Athlete*, with the runners taken from a photograph, was painted with an air brush. *Homer* was a redesigned label which he did after looking at a similar label produced earlier by another artist.

Additional examples of his work which appear in this book include *Cascade O' Gold* (page 59), *Marquita* (page 62), *Co-Ed* (page 63), and *Cowboy* (page 69). He also designed large numbers of lemon, pear, apple, grape and vegetable box labels. In his spare time and since his retirement Ted Clark also painted fine art oil paintings of many different subjects which he has exhibited and sold.

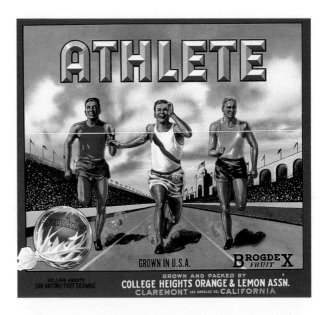

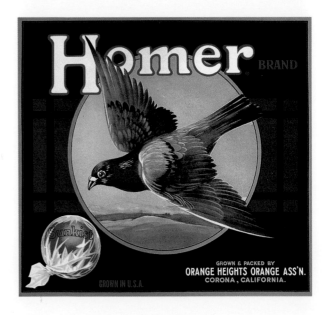

99

Walter Clark

Walter was the eldest of the three Clark brothers and the first to move to San Francisco. He had both artistic and trade experience before emigrating, so it was easy for him to get work when he arrived. From 1921 to 1960 he was primarily a freelance artist and very active as a label designer, working mostly for San Francisco lithograph firms. *Air Mail* is a sample of the work he did in the 1920's.

Dario De Julio

Dario De Julio was born and raised in the vineyard area near Ontario, California, the son of a chemist who worked for a large winery. After attending art school in Los Angeles in the 1930's, he became a freelance artist, designing advertisements and titles for the movie industry. Like many artists who had commercial art training in the 1930's, he specialized in bold lettering combined with colorful airbrush graphics.

He joined Western Lithograph in 1938, where he worked as a staff artist for 20 years, interrupted by service as an Air Force pilot for periods in the 1940's and 1950's. In 1958 he became art director for Western Lithograph, a position he held for several years before starting a successful freelance business in Los Angeles.

In addition to the labels shown here, the *Circle* series (page 55) is an example of his work. In fact, these were the first labels he designed after joining Western. *Mentone* (page 57) is another example of his use of airbrush techniques.

100

J. Frank Derby

J. Frank Derby was born in Plymouth, Pennsylvania in 1875. As a young man he moved to Los Angeles where he studied art at several schools. Around 1900 he designed posters and labels for the Los Angeles Lithograph Company. After Union Lithograph bought them out, he continued to work there for several more years and then became chief of the design staff at the Western Lithograph Company. He worked there for 20 years as a poster artist and label designer. *Orange Queen*, *Selects* and *Mercury* are among his best known designs; many others were of similar high quality. Some labels he designed, including the first two listed above, appeared on posters and program covers for the Orange Show in San Bernardino, a large well attended winter festival where each packing house exhibited elaborate displays of fruit and promoted their individual brands. In addition, he produced covers for the *Citrograph*, the key industry trade journal. He also designed advertisements for Western Lithograph which appeared in industry publications.

During the years he spent at Western he had the unique opportunity to study posters from all over the world, which the firm's owner had collected while traveling. There is no doubt those posters inspired him and other Western artists to produce high quality work.

By the late 1920's he was pursuing a freelance commercial career and exhibiting his fine art paintings in shows around Southern California. Aside from his talent as a painter and graphic designer he also composed many semi-classical and romantic musical works.

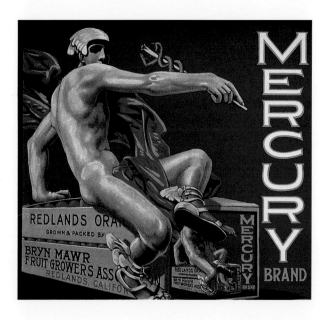

101

Charles J. Dickman

Charles Dickman came to San Francisco from Germany where he was born in 1863. In 1884 he was an artist at the A.L. Bancroft Company. In 1886 he and two partners formed the Dickman-Jones-Hettrick Lithograph Company, which later became Dickman-Jones. For about 10 years they produced high quality stone lithographed labels, many of which initiated design formats that were used heavily by other label artists in future years.

After Mutual Label and Lithography bought Dickman-Jones in 1898, Dickman went to Paris where he took formal art instruction from Constant and Lourens. He then returned to California and lived in Monterey, where he established himself as a fine art painter of local landscapes, exhibiting his works in galleries and museums. *Date Palm* and *Angel* are examples of his work while in the lithographic trade.

Henry F. Gorham

In the early 1890's Henry Gorham began working as an artist at the H.S. Crocker Lithograph Company. By 1896 he was at the Dickman-Jones Lithograph Company, and from the turn of the century until the 1906 earthquake he worked at the Mutual Label and Lithography Company. Later, he was a freelance artist in San Francisco, until 1915 when he took a permanent job at the Schmidt Lithography Company. There he and C.A. Beck set up an elaborate art department in the penthouse on top of the Schmidt factory, high above the San Francisco skyline.

Throughout his long career Gorham produced thousands of labels of all sorts, many of which were for the California citrus industry. He was active at a time when stone lithographed versions of labels were being done, and also is credited with producing outstanding examples of the later tempera and watercolor illustrations. *Yokohl* is an example of the type of label he did in the early period and *Belle of Piru* represents his later work.

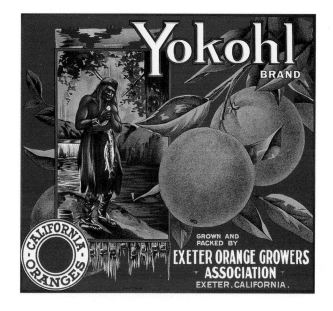

Carl Hague

Carl Hague and his family moved to the San Francisco area while he was still a young boy. When he was 18, he began attending "Brino's School." After several years there, he joined the Schmidt Lithography Company for a few years. During the mid 1930's he operated a freelance art studio with Mickey O'Shea in San Francisco. Together they designed many box labels for the major lithograph firms.

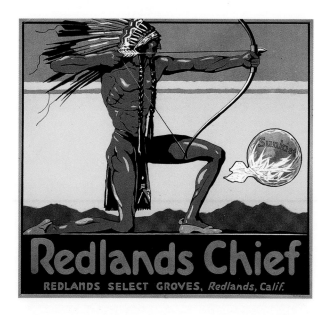

H.W. Hansen

After studying art in Germany and England, Herman Hansen emigrated to the United States. He took further art instruction at the Chicago Art Institute and did commercial art work for several years. In the 1880's he moved to San Francisco and began working for the H.S. Crocker Lithograph Company as a staff artist. There his watercolor paintings were reproduced as advertisements for various California products. A number were used for citrus labels.

In 1898 he quit working for Crocker, operated a freelance art studio for several

103

years, and then worked full time as a fine art painter of Western scenes. Many of these were classics featuring cowboys, Indians and horses, all of which he liked to paint and which he did very well. His paintings were exhibited and sold on the east coast and in Europe, as well as locally. *Polo* is a typical example of his early commercial work, while *Advance* features a subject that is very much like his fine art produced in later years. He also did the illustration for the original *Bronco* label (page 14).

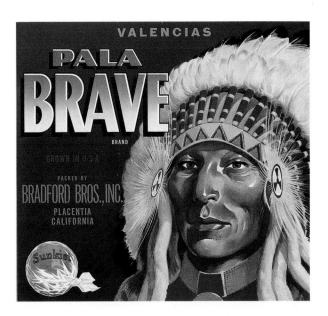

Bill Law

About 1940 a Scotsman named Bill Law began working at Western Lithograph. He had studied art in Canada and was very good at painting with an air brush. He specialized in producing vignettes of fruit and full figure illustrations; he did little lettering. He painted the Indian head on *Pala Brave*; the lettering was done by another staff artist. He worked at Western until the 1950's.

Felix Martini

For about 12 years beginning in the late 1920's Felix Martini worked at the Western Lithograph Company as an illustrator. He painted almost exclusively with regular brushes and usually used tempera paints or watercolors. His label illustrations included a wide variety of subjects ranging from landscapes and still lifes to human figures and animals. He did little lettering.

In his spare time Mr. Martini traveled around California making oil paintings of rural landscapes and ''thumb nail sketches,'' which he kept on file at Western. Often these sketches were used to produce labels like *Highland Grove*. They also were used for some of the many stock label designs he produced while working there. The bird illustration on *Gorgeous* is a good example of his treatment of this type of subject. It was probably done shortly after he joined the Western Lithograph Company.

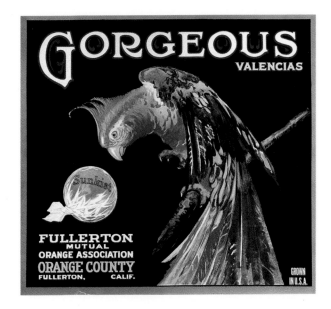

Othello Michetti

Othello Michetti came to America from Italy with his family about 1905. After attending high school in New York he studied at the Art Students League and the Academy of Design, while working for the Cusack Outdoor Advertising Company. In 1918 he moved to San Jose, California and began working at the Murrison Label Company, designing can labels. About 1921 he was hired to establish an art department at the Traung Label and Lithography Company, and became its first art director.

In his spare time he painted in water colors. Some of his paintings were translated into label designs; others were exhibited in art galleries and in museum shows. He was able to accurately paint the human figure, animals, birds, still lifes, or whatever the job called for.

He was a leading figure in the label design field. He gave lectures on the application of modern design and color to labels, and wrote a booklet on the subject entitled *Color Harmony*.

Charlie Nittle

Charlie Nittle grew up in Wisconsin where he was born in 1886. He attended the Chicago Art Institute in 1914, then worked at a local lithograph firm in Chicago. There he learned the trade and worked full time as a designer of large stone lithographed posters for theatrical events, circuses, and food products.

He moved to San Francisco in the early 1920's and worked for the H.S. Crocker Lithograph Company. Several years later he moved to Los Angeles where he was art director for the Union Lithograph Company. In this position he designed labels for many products including citrus box labels, while continuing to work as a poster designer. In the 1940's he worked as an artist for the Neuner Lithograph Company, and then did freelance commercial art work until the early 1950's. He then worked at the Western Lithograph Company for several years.

Nittle produced his finest box label designs between the late 1920's and the mid 1940's. He was able to incorporate an artistic look typical of the oil paint illustration style taught at the Chicago Art Institute. *Grandeur* (page 91) is an example. He also applied the flat graphic style used on posters, which he had learned while working in that field, on such labels as *Vigilant, Hopi* and *Chinese Girl. Celebration* (page 53) is another example of his work.

As is the case with most of the commercial artists discussed here, he produced fine art paintings in addition to his label designs. Most of these were oils on canvas, many depicting seascape views of the California coastline.

Godfrey Nystrom

About 1920 Godfrey Nystrom moved from Sweden to San Francisco with his family. After attending ''Brino's School,'' he worked at the Western Lithograph Company from 1929 to 1931, at Crocker-Union in San Francisco from 1931 to 1934, and then went back to Los Angeles where he did freelance work and was employed by the Union Lithograph Company for several years. He was active as a label box designer during this period. *Legal Tender* is an example of his work.

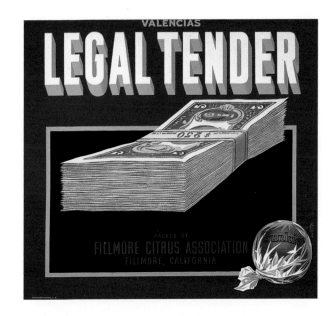

Claude Putnam

From 1920 to about 1945 Claude Putnam or ''PUT,'' as he sometimes signed his work, was a commercial artist in Los Angeles. He designed all types of packaging labels, book illustrations, maps and greeting cards. He also produced a comic strip named ''The Salome Frog.'' One of his most popular art treatments was produced by using an ink and water process to create a wood block style, as on *Honeymoon*. It is also quite possible he designed *California Dream* (page 52).

Archie J. Vazquez

Archie Vazquez was the son of immigrants from the Basque area between France and Spain. His first commercial art jobs were sheet music cover design, and as an artist at the Los Angeles Engraving Company. He joined the Western Lithograph Company in 1918, where he was art director of the sketch department until 1956. During this period, he was one of the most prolific artists in the field of citrus label design.

Most of his original sketches were painted with watercolors. He seemed comfortable with illustrating virtually any

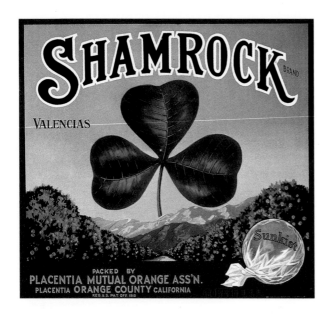

subject, and was also an exceptionally good lettering artist. His versatility enabled him to do complete label designs. Vazquez was very interested in color combinations and their effect on the viewer. His constant experiments with unusual tonal values led to a booklet on the subject which he wrote and illustrated in the 1940's, called *Color Illusions*.

Those that worked for him remember him as a disciplined, extremely hard working individual who expected the same from artists he hired. Each artist worked in a separate area divided by frosted glass; no talking was allowed. While these working conditions were rigid, no one can argue with the results. His art department consistently produced high quality innovative designs.

Western Queen, *Shamrock*, *Tesoro Rancho* and *La Reina*, are examples of his work.

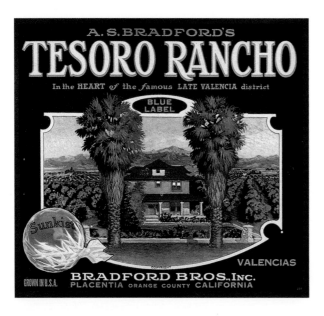

In addition to the art directors and artists discussed here, a listing is given of other artists known to have worked on label designs, but for whom no biographical information is available.

Additional Label Artists

Morton Addy	Western Lithograph	Graphic Artist	1920's-30's
Fred Allen	Western Lithograph	Lettering Artist	1920's-50's
Alex Andres	Olsen Brothers	Graphic Artist	1930's
Arnold Armitage	Western Lithograph	Graphic Artist	1930's-50's
Frank Baird	Western Lithograph	Lettering Artist	1920's-50's
Frank Beltran	Western Lithograph	Graphic Artist	1950's
John Coolidge	Freelance (L.A.)	Graphic Artist	1920's
Guy Parker Goodwin	Freelance (L.A.)	Graphic Artist	1920's
Kurt W. Graichen	Western Lithograph	Engraver	1920's-30's
Harold Gretzner	Schmidt Lithograph	Graphic Artist	1930's-50's
Claude Grapentine	Traung Lithograph	Engraver	1920's
Frank F. Green	Freelance (L.A.)	Graphic Artist	1920's
Allen Hall	Western Lithograph	Graphic Artist	1950's
Thomas Harter	Western Lithograph	Graphic Artist	1920's
Stanley Ilsley	Western Lithograph	Graphic Artist	1930's
John Juliani	Freelance (S.F.)	Graphic Artist	1930's-50's
Eric Karger	Union Lithograph (L.A.)	Engraver	1930's
Fred Methner	Traung Lithograph	Graphic Artist	1930's
Mickey O'Shea	Freelance (S.F.)	Graphic Artist	1930's-40's
Morri Ovsey	Western Lithograph	Graphic Artist	1930's
Clyde Provancia	Western Lithograph	Graphic Artist	1950's
Gordon Provancia	Western Lithograph	Graphic Artist	1950's
Lewis Rothe	Freelance (L.A.)	Graphic Artist	1920's-30's
Rudy Schmidt	Schmidt Lithograph	Graphic Artist	1920's-30's
Leon Sharmon	Schmidt Lithograph	Graphic Artist	1930's
Bill Sperry	Freelance (S.F.)	Graphic Artist	1920's-30's
Louis Sturm	Schmidt Lithograph	Graphic Artist	1930's
Lynol White	Western Lithograph	Graphic Artist	1950's
Jud Wright	Freelance (L.A.)	Graphic Artist	1920's

CHAPTER VI
LABEL LITHOGRAPHERS

The growth and development of the orange label lithographic industry followed a pattern common in industrial America. The industry was started by entrepreneurs and was small and fragmented when the first labels were used in the 1880's. As the need for labels grew and increasingly sophisticated label design and production techniques were used, the industry gradually became consolidated in the hands of a few leaders who had developed efficient production facilities and superior marketing organizations.

Over 35 companies were involved at one time or another in orange box label production during the 70 year period of label use, as listed on page 116. A large percentage of the labels, however, were produced by three companies—the

Schmidt Lithograph Company, the Western Lithograph Company and, in later years, the Carton Label Company.

Max Schmidt was the key figure in the early development of the California label industry. He was born in northern Germany in 1850, went to sea as a cabin boy at 14, and arrived in San Francisco in 1871. He held a number of short term jobs with various San Francisco printing and engraving companies. In 1873 a relative of his in Germany sent him a description of a new zinc etching process for making printing plates, called zincography, developed to replace the slow and expensive wood engraving techniques in use at the time to produce plates for newspaper illustrations.

He went into business to produce plates using his new zinc etching process, and soon was the plate supplier for all the San Francisco newspapers. He then began to design and print stock certificates and wine labels, and in the 1880's began to produce box and can labels for the developing fruit, vegetable, and salmon packing industries.

A second pioneer in the California label industry was the H.S. Crocker Company, started by Henry Crocker in 1856 as a job printing company in Sacramento. He moved to San Francisco in 1871 and began to lithograph stock certificates and business documents. His company grew rapidly and by 1886, when it began major production of orange box labels, employed 150 people in a five story plant.

In 1885 Charles Dickman and George Jones, an artist and an engraver at the A.L. Bancroft Company, joined Michael Hettrick to form the Dickman-Jones-Hettrick Company. The firm, renamed the Dickman-Jones Company in 1888, produced high quality well designed orange box labels, and produced the initial de-

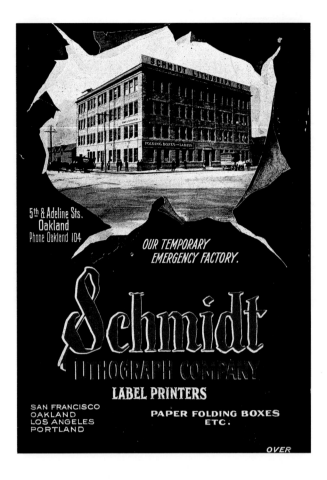

signs of many labels that continued to be used in revised form for many years.

Three other lithograph firms that would be active in the label business for many years were established in San Francisco in the 1880's. J.C. Hall of Providence, Rhode Island, started J.C. Hall & Co., renamed Union Lithography in 1890. The Galloway Lithograph Co. was started by William T. Galloway and Otto Schoning; and, Louis Roesch started a company bearing his name. Also, the A.L. Bancroft company, in business since the late 1860's, began label production.

In Los Angeles, the Los Angeles Lithograph Co. was started in the 1880's, with Theodore A. Schmidt as president. Shortly before 1900, the Western Lithograph Co. was formed with Anton E. Stoetzer, a former fresco painter, as manager.

In 1899 Max Schmidt took the leadership of the San Francisco label lithograph industry by acquiring Dickman-Jones and the lithograph department of H.S. Crocker. He named his new firm the Mutual Label and Lithographic Co., and became the major label supplier. Los Angeles Lithograph and Western Lithograph were also associated with Mutual for brief periods in the early 1900's.

In the 1890's and early 1900's a number of orange box labels were lithographed by midwestern and eastern firms. The main eastern producer was Stecher Lithograph in Rochester, New York, a major printer of catalogs, posters, and labels for the Rochester seed and packing industries. Other label lithographers were the Denver Lithograph Company; the Calvert Lithograph Company in Detroit; Woodward Tiernan and the Gast Lithograph Company in St. Louis; the American Lithograph Company, the Gray Lithograph Company, McLaughlin Brothers and Albert Datz in New York; the United States Printing Company in Brooklyn; the

Boston Bank Note Company; and the Maryland Color Printing Company in Baltimore.

The San Francisco lithography industry was completely destroyed in the 1906 earthquake and fire. All production equipment, label designs, and business records were lost. The disaster was a double blow for Union Lithography. Their plant had burned down early in 1906, was quickly rebuilt and in operation in March, and was destroyed again in the April earthquake.

The industry immediately began to rebuild. Max Schmidt bought the Wempe Box Company in Oakland, where he produced labels until his new facility was rebuilt in San Francisco. He gave up the Mutual name, and called his firm the Schmidt Lithograph Company.

Union Lithograph bought the Los Angeles Lithograph Company. Their press work was done in Los Angeles, from designs made in various studios in San Francisco, Oakland, and Chicago.

After the disruption caused by the earthquake, a number of new firms were started in San Francisco. Olov E. Olson, formerly employed by the Galloway Lithograph Company, formed the O.E. Olson Company. Arthur Pingree and Adam Brengel, a pressman at Mutual, formed the Pingree-Brengel Company.

Western Lithograph was acquired by Warren Gilbert and William Jones in 1907, and renamed the Gilbert-Jones-Rugg Co. After a year, in a most unusual business transaction, Jones traded his interest in the firm to Milton L. Davidson, for Davidson's Montana ranch. Under Davidson's direction the firm, renamed Western Lithograph, began large scale production of labels, along with posters, advertising cards, business forms, and billboards.

In 1912 the identical twin brothers Louis and Charles Traung, supervisors at

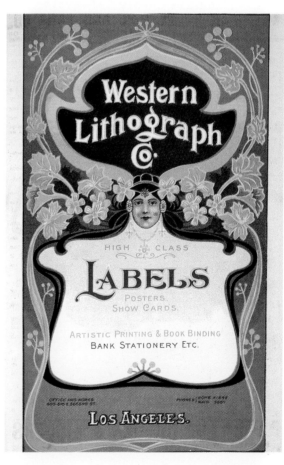

Schmidt Lithography for many years, became associated with Pingree-Brengel and reorganized it as Pingre-Traung, with Charles Traung as president.

In 1916 they renamed the firm the Traung Label and Lithograph Company. The firm rapidly became a leader in label production, with high quality designs and technically advanced production techniques. While they never produced the quantity of orange box labels that were produced by Schmidt and Western, they became the leaders in the production of labels for other agricultural products such as apples, pears, grapes, and vegetables.

The H.S. Crocker company was purchased by new owners in 1919, who also bought the Union Lithograph Company in 1922. For several years, the two companies kept their respective identities, maintaining separate sales forces. About 1920 the Schwabacher-Frey Company, San Francisco stationers and printers since the early 1900's, began to lithograph orange box labels.

Two new firms, specializing in low cost production, entered the label business in the early 1920's. Adolph Lehmann, active in the commercial printing business since 1901, began large scale production of stock labels for the citrus, canning and wine industries. He maintained a huge inventory of stock labels, and could supply labels quickly and cheaply. In the mid 1930's he claimed in advertisements that he had 100 million labels in stock.

The other new arrival was the Carton Label Company, founded by F.W. Shean and Louis A. Miller. They set out to be an aggressive low cost designer and producer of labels. As cost pressures continued to increase during the depression years of the 1930's, they became a major label producer.

In the late 1920's and early 1930's offset printing replaced the earlier stone and metal plate lithography, a technical change that helped consolidate label production in the hands of a few strong companies. A key event was the development of a four color press in 1931 by Louis Traung, which would print labels in one operation without the need for drying the ink between the various color printings.

In the mid-1930's Traung was bought by Stecher in Rochester, and the firm renamed Stecher-Traung, with their main production facilities in San Francisco. Crocker and Union formally combined to form Crocker-Union in 1936, and then readopted the original H.S. Crocker name in 1946. The firm is still active in the lithography business in the San Francisco area.

With the abrupt end of the orange label business in the mid-1950's, the lithograph industry became consolidated in a few large companies. Western was bought by Brown-Bigelow in 1953. Carton Label was bought by Security Printing in the mid-1950's, which was then acquired by Diamond International. They also acquired Schwabacher Frey.

In 1966 a final consolidation took place, when Stecher-Traung acquired Schmidt, combining three of the great names in the label business into one company— Stecher, Traung & Schmidt.

The companies that lithographed orange box labels are listed on page 116, along with the approximate dates when they were actively printing labels. In some cases, the firm name was used for a short period after it was acquired by another company. While many firms had sales offices in several cities, their headquarters and main production facilities were in the cities listed here.

The San Francisco lithographic industry underwent a steady series of mergers and consolidations. A general outline of the major changes that took place is shown on page 117.

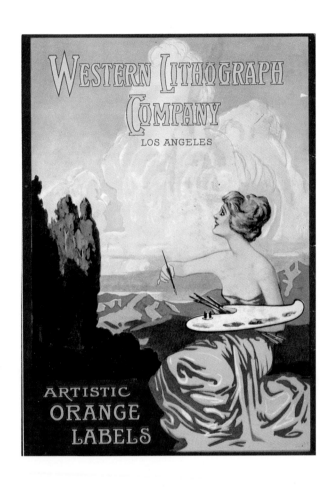

Orange Box Label Lithographers

American Litho. Co.	New York	ca. 1900
Boston Bank Note Co.	Boston	ca. 1900
Britton & Rey	San Francisco	ca. 1900
Calvert Litho. Co.	Detroit	ca. 1900
Carton Label Co.	San Francisco	1927-1955
H.S. Crocker Co. (old)	San Francisco	1885-1899
H.S. Crocker Co. (new)	San Francisco	1948-1955
Crocker-Union	San Francisco	1936-1948
Denver Litho. Co.	Denver	ca. 1900
Dickman-Jones Co.	San Francisco	1888-1899
Galloway Litho. Co.	San Francisco	1885-1935
Gast Litho. Co.	St. Louis	ca. 1900
Gilbert-Jones-Rugg Co.	Los Angeles	1907-1908
Gray Litho. Co.	New York	ca. 1900
Halpin Litho. Co.	San Francisco	1915-1930
Los Angeles Litho. Co.	Los Angeles	1890-1906
Maryland Color Printing Co.	Baltimore	ca. 1900
Miller Litho. Co.	San Francisco	1925-1933
McLaughlin Bros.	New York	ca. 1900
Mutual Label and Litho. Co.	San Francisco	1920-1935
Olson Litho. Co.	San Francisco	1909-1929
Olson Bros. Litho. Co.	San Francisco	1929-1955
Pingree-Traung	San Francisco	1912-1915
George Rice & Sons	Los Angeles	ca. 1900
Louis Roesch & Co.	San Francisco	1920-1955
Schmidt Label & Litho. Co.	San Francisco	1885-1899
Schmidt Litho. Co.	San Francisco	1906-1955
Schwabacher-Frey	San Francisco	1920-1955
Smith-Barnes Co.	Los Angeles	1920-1934
Stecher Litho. Co.	Rochester	1895-1910
Stecher-Traung Litho. Co.	San Francisco	1934-1955
Traung Label & Litho. Co.	San Francisco	1916-1934
Union Litho. Co.	San Francisco	1885-1936
Union Litho. Co.	Los Angeles	1906-1936
United States Printing Co.	Brooklyn	ca. 1900
Western Litho. Co.	Los Angeles	1900-1955
Woodward & Tiernan	St. Louis	ca. 1900

San Francisco Lithographers

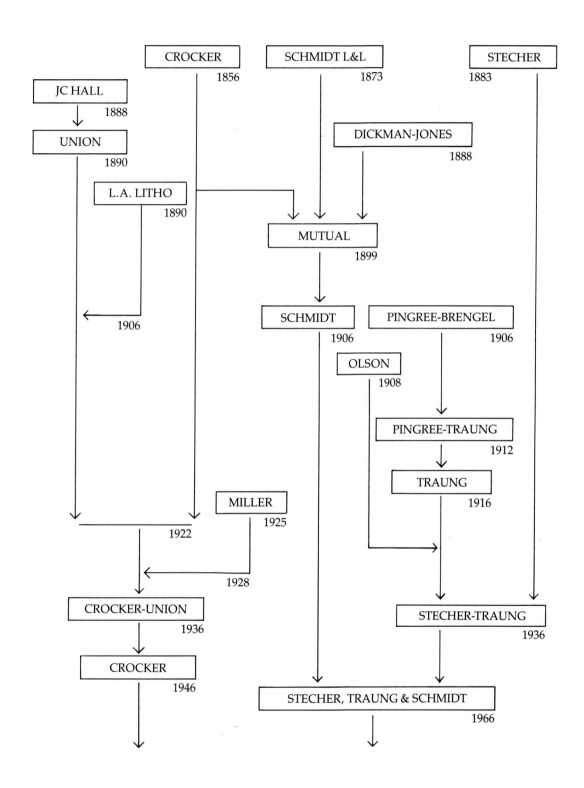

CROCKER 1856

SCHMIDT L&L 1873

STECHER 1883

JC HALL 1888

UNION 1890

DICKMAN-JONES 1888

L.A. LITHO 1890

MUTUAL 1899

1906

SCHMIDT 1906

PINGREE-BRENGEL 1906

OLSON 1908

PINGREE-TRAUNG 1912

TRAUNG 1916

MILLER 1925

1922

1928

CROCKER-UNION 1936

STECHER-TRAUNG 1936

CROCKER 1946

STECHER, TRAUNG & SCHMIDT 1966

CHAPTER VII
LITHOGRAPHY

The basic techniques of lithography—printing from a perfectly flat stone onto a sheet of paper pressed against the stone—were discovered in 1798 by Aloys Senefelder, a Bavarian artist. Throughout the 1800's many commercial organizations improved the process to make lithography suitable for low cost color reproduction.

By the 1880's American chromolithographers had developed the process into a nationwide business, making it technically and commercially feasible for orange growers to use large full-color labels for their box ends. Although many printers had special trade secrets that gave their product a unique look, they all used the same basic procedures.

The basic lithographic process involves drawing an im-

119

age in grease, with a pencil or crayon, on a perfectly flat block of limestone. When the greased stone is dampened with water, ink will stick to the greased areas and be repelled by the watered, ungreased areas. When a sheet of paper is pressed against the surface, the image will be transferred from the inked greased areas to the paper.

For color lithography, a series of stones is used, each containing one color of the desired final image. The composite lithograph is produced by sequentially printing the image from each stone onto a sheet of paper.

For orange label production in the early days, a watercolor sketch of the desired label was first made by a label artist and approved by the customer. The plate maker then traced an outline drawing of the sketch onto a gelatine sheet, and transferred this keyline drawing onto the polished surfaces of as many stones as there were colors to be printed. After a careful study of the watercolor sketch, the appropriate areas of each of the color stones would be filled in, so when the set of plates was printed the composite image would be an accurate copy of the original.

The most common set of colors used consisted of red, pink, dark blue, light blue, and yellow. Green and black were rarely used as they could easily be produced by color superposition.

The key problems for accurate color reproduction were the production of identical keyline images on each of the color stones, the skill required to fill in the appropriate areas on each stone to produce the desired final image, quality control of the ink formulations, and accurate re-registration when the color images were sequentially transferred from the stone to the label being lithographed.

The stone plates were heavy and cumbersome, weighing up to several hundred pounds, and were easily broken. In the 1900's the use of stone plates was gradually superseded by thin zinc or aluminum plates, when it was found that these metal surfaces could be treated and polished to form the same high quality color images as the stones.

Finally, a thinner version of the metal sheet was used which was bent into a curved form and attached to a cylindrical roller, leading to a more efficient rotary process.

In order to print a large number of images from the lithograph plate, the inked impression usually was transferred onto the surface of an intermediate rubber roller, and then from the roller onto the sheet of paper. This offset process enabled the original basic plates to be used for long periods of time without deterioration of the original greased image.

In the late 1920's, the set of color separation plates began to be made by photographic techniques, and used in multicolor offset presses. This is the basic process still in use today.

The schematic progression on the next page shows the development of the label lithographic process. Stone plates were used from the 1880's until the 1920's. Zinc or aluminum plates were introduced as a substitute about 1900 and gradually replaced stones over the next 25 years. Both stone and metal plates usually were used with offset rollers. Photo-offset lithography began to be used in the late 1920's, rapidly becoming the dominant production process.

Lithographic Plate Evolution

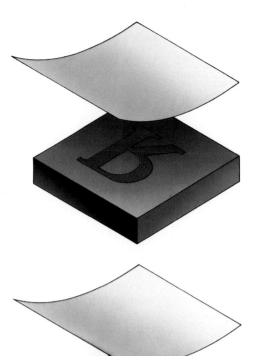

Stone Lithography
Paper pressed against the inked surface of the stone

Metal Plate Lithography
Stone replaced with a zinc or aluminum plate

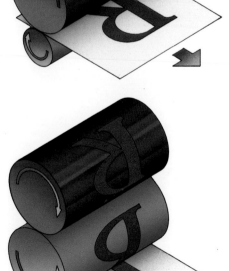

Cylindrical roller lithography
Plate curved onto a cylinder

Offset lithography
Image transferred to an intermediate offset rubber roller

Paper fed between rollers.

Crayon Drawing

The earliest color lithographs were made up of solid blocks of primary colors, placed side by side. To produce the complete color spectrum, techniques were developed to intermingle small color areas, which the eye interpreted as a composite color. These small color areas were first produced by drawing directly on the lithographic stone with a crayon or grease pencil. Great skill and experience was needed to get the correct color combinations and accurate placement of the grease patterns to achieve the range of hues and tints needed for a pleasing naturalistic final image.

Color intensity was determined by the pressure of the crayon on the stone—the harder the stone was pressed, the darker the color. The lithographic stone was usually prepared with a finely grained surface to give maximum control over the crayon.

For all label production it was, of course, an essential requirement that the orange be a vibrant color. This was usually achieved by printing light red over yellow, and then shading by incorporating small red crayon areas. The density of red near the edge was increased to give a shadowed appearance, which would make the orange appear round.

A section of an orange produced by crayon lithographic techniques is shown, along with sections from the *Prospector* stock label (page 35) and from *Riverside* (page 4).

Hand Stippling

To produce finer color resolution and better control of color gradations, arrays of small stippled dots were used in addition to the relatively crude crayon patterns. By 1900, stippling had replaced crayon drawing for most label plate production. Correct intermingling of the dot patterns led to a more accurate rendition of the original artist's sketch than had been possible with the earlier techniques.

Hand stippling was very tedious and time-consuming. An apprentice lithograph stone artist spent long hours practicing his stippling techniques. A skilled stippler produced dot patterns in the form of smoothly flowing curved arcs, giving a pleasing texture to the stippled areas.

In order to speed up the stippling process, special tools with a number of tips were used, to put down an array of dots in one operation.

Stippled dots of carefully controlled size were necessary to produce an attractive pattern. Instead of the grained stone used for crayon work, the stone used for the stippled image was highly polished to give the lithographic plate artist greater control over the stippling process.

To illustrate hand stippling, details are shown from *Angel* (page 102) and *Atta Boy* (page 44). The placement of red dots to produce a natural appearing orange are also shown.

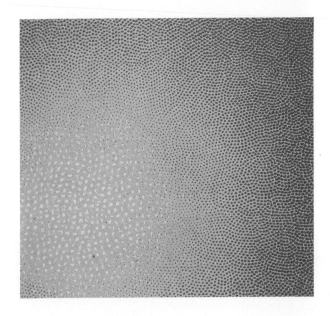

Ben Day Screens

To remove some of the drudgery from hand stippling, around 1900 Benjamin Day, a New York lithographer, invented a screen process for depositing arrays of dots.

The Ben Day screen was a transparent gelatin-like sheet held in a frame. The upper surface of the screen was smooth, the bottom surface containing an array of small raised dots. The dot pattern was lightly greased, and the screen held a small distance above the stone. By lightly pressing on the screen, the greased dot pattern was transferred to the stone.

By carefully masking the area to be covered with dots, and by the use of proper techniques to avoid smudging, large areas of labels could be quickly and effectively filled with dot patterns.

Over 100 different Ben Day screen patterns were available by the 1920's, when the process was most widely used for label production. Some hand stippling was almost always used in conjunction with Ben Day dot deposition to make gradual image transitions.

Examples of Ben Day stippling are shown on sections from *Tropic* (page 43) and *Good Cheer* (page 40). The regular stippled pattern on the orange here can be compared with the hand stippled pattern on the previous page.

Half-tones

A revolution took place in the late 1920's and early 1930's with the introduction of photographic techniques for label production. Instead of producing sets of stone or metal plates, the original art work was photographed through a set of color filters, and the color separation plates produced by further photographic techniques.

When the art was photographed, a half-tone plate consisting of an array of closely spaced dots was placed slightly in front of the photographic plate. The final photo-lithograph plates thus consisted of patterns formed of arrays of very small dots.

This permitted very accurate color reproduction. A standard screen used 120 dots per linear inch, about 15,000 dots per square inch, over ten times the dot density possible with the most sophisticated stippling techniques.

The new half-tone process eliminated the need for the lithographic artist. The production of lithograph plates from the artist's drawing became a straightforward photomechanical operation.

The half-tone process greatly decreased the cost of label production, especially when the labels were printed in large four color presses which would print the colors in a continuous operation, without the need of drying the inked image between the various color runs.

Examples of half-tone printing are shown on sections from *Pacoast* (page 96) and *Co-Ed* (page 63).

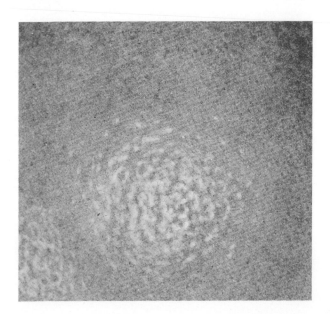

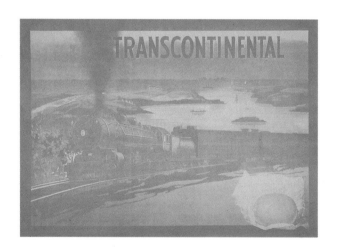

The set of proofs from color separation plates used to lithograph a label in the 1930's is shown here, consisting of dark blue, two shades of light blue, red, pink, and yellow.

As can be seen above in the final composite image, the entire color spectrum is reproduced by the appropriate superposition of these colors.

LABEL DATING

The dating of labels is far from an exact science. In addition to the problem of determining when the label was originally designed, it may have been printed years or even decades later, sometimes with subtle design modifications.

A key indication of label age is the choice of label subject and the way it is treated in label design, as discussed in the chapters on Naturalism, Advertising, and Commercial Art. Design techniques incorporating crayon drawing, hand stippling, or Ben Day stippling provide some indication of age, but this is complicated by the fact that a combination of techniques were usually used on the same label. A more reliable indication of label age is the use of half-tone lithography, a technique rarely used before 1930, but the dominant production method a few years later.

Many lithographers printed their firm name on the bottom of the label, which can be used in conjunction with the information on pages 116 and 117 to help determine label age.

A very useful age indication is the three or four digit code on the bottom of most Western Lithograph labels, giving the month and year the label was printed. The label, however, could have been designed considerably before the specific example was printed.

Dating is also helped by knowing when the various label trademarks and logos were first used. The *Sunkist* trademark was introduced in 1907, the Sunburst logo in 1908 (page 14), and the logo employing straight line lettering in a simple circle in 1917 (page 70). Both of these logos were gradually replaced by various modifications of the wrapped orange logo, starting in 1917. The *Red Ball* trademark was introduced in 1911, with the familiar red logo (page 88) first used about 1920.

The Mutual *Pure Gold* trademark was introduced in 1910, with the cross design (page 88) and the *Silver Seal* logo first used in 1924. The American Fruit Growers *Blue Goose* trademark was introduced in 1918, with the standard solid design (page 89) first used in 1925.

The trademarks of various chemical and waxing techniques for preserving fruit during shipment are sometimes included on labels. These include *Brodgex* (page 38), first used in 1921, and *Flavorseal* (page 65), in 1939.

An accurate but time consuming method of determining when a label was printed is knowing when a specific packer or shipper used his name on the label. This can be learned by referring to city directories and industry trade journals and records.

By taking into account a combination of these criteria, and by the experience gained by looking at a large number of labels, reasonably accurate estimations of label age can be made.

ACKNOWLEDGMENTS

The authors are deeply indebted to many individuals who were generous with their time during interviews, and with information regarding label design and production. A number of rare labels were also located with their help. We wish to thank the following:

Adrian Apple, Ralph Baker, August Bissiri, Ray Bjorklund, Karl Bornstein, Veronica Chiang, Al Clark, Ted Clark, Walter Clark, Debby Cullins, John Davidson, Dario De Julio, Charline Divine, Louis Drago, Clyde Fairburn, Tom Fay, Jack Ford, Dorothy Gleason, Laurie Gordon, Rick Griffin, Carl Hague, Alan Hall, Levi Hirschler, Ron Jones, John Juliani, Esther Klotz, William Leonard, Jim and Linda Mackie, Louise and Othello Michetti, Godfrey Nystrom, Richard Opsitos, Jack Overall, Bud Roberts, Ed Salter, Brenda Shook, Jim Sleeper, Ray Soper, Harold Swanson, Frank Tesch, Mark Trout, Deiter Vielhauer, John Yaros and Lyonel White.

The staffs at Sunkist Growers, Inc., and at Mutual Orange Distributors also generously provided help and useful information, as did members of the Citrus Label Society, Riverside, California. The Doctoral thesis of Josephine Kingsbury Jacobs (UCLA, 1966) was useful for information on the development of Sunkist advertising, as was Rahno Mabel MacCurdy's book, *The History of the California Fruit Exchange* (Los Angeles, 1925).

Photographs of label artists were kindly supplied by Dario De Julio and Godfrey Nystrom.

Many libraries helped to provide needed information. These include the library at the Los Angeles County Museum of Art; the Los Angeles Public Library; the Pomona Public Library; the San Francisco Public Library; the Sherman Foundation; the Bancroft Library at the University of California, Berkeley; and the Research Library at the University of California, Los Angeles.

Finally, the authors wish to express their gratitude to Deborah Last and Debi McClelland for their help and encouragement over the long period during which this book was being written.

INDEX